WHAT
IS ENOUGH

To Alexis,
I pray this Book is a
Blessing to you.
07/03/20

WHAT IS ENOUGH:

"How to Lighten Your Load & Find *What* Makes You Happy"

Copyright © 2019 Treveal C.W. Lynch

West Bound Publishing

ISBN (print): 978-1-7337233-0-5
ISBN (ebook): 978-1-7337233-1-2
Printed in the United States of America.

WHAT
IS ENOUGH

How to Lighten Your Load and
Find What Makes You Happy

TREVEAL C.W. LYNCH

DEDICATION

Pastor Eric Brown of Pasadena Church
(In His Loving Memory)

This book is dedicated to a man who looked me in the eye 17 years ago and told me WHAT I was. It was simple, yet profound, and completely life-changing.

My wife and I had recently relocated to southern California and had been members of Pasadena Church for only one year when I was given an opportunity to share a 15-minute lesson on the life of Jesus to a group of men from our congregation.

As I gathered my things near the front of the stage, Pastor Eric leaned over to me and put a hand on my shoulder. We locked eyes, and he said the four most important words I had ever heard: "*Treveal, you're a teacher.*" He paused, as if to allow his words to soak in, before smiling and walking away.

In that moment, I felt informed, inspired and intrigued, all at the same time. From that moment on, learning more about **what** I was became a passion and later proved to be the centerpiece of my purpose. I was completely captivated by discovering how I could be useful as a gift from God, and I began a journey that has brought me to this very place and time in my life.

Eric didn't have to tell me what he saw in me that night. He could have second guessed himself (or me), but he didn't. Thank God, he didn't. Eric was courageous, caring, confident, and centered. He was the greatest thing he could have possibly been in that moment: He was **being what** he was in the very likeness and image of the Creator.

Thanks to you, Pastor Eric, today I'm free to be **what** I am because you showed me you were free to be **what** you were. I love you, respect you, and thank you for **being** this most precious gift.

FOREWORD

By Pastor Madelyn D. Manning,
Co-Pastor of Pasadena Church...the church with no limits

"Are you tired of where you are?"

"Do you want to change?"

"Do you want your life to be better?"

The sound response to these questions is what initiated the fascinating remaking of my spiritual son, Treveal C. W. Lynch. In this compelling book, he has done something that I believe will guide you to your own irrefutable transformation.

It's amazing to me how his one encounter with a woman in a sauna set the scene for a powerful explanation of the perfectionist culture we live in that leaves us exhausted, empty and deflated. Because he has been "there," Treveal opens up his life experiences in a way that draws us in and many times I found myself saying, "Yes, that's me." Furthermore, he offers hope by sharing with us how he changed his life for the better through a profound loving relationship that forever marked him as being "Enough."

Within every human being is the desire for significance - the quality of your life's meaning and purpose being seen as important, taken seriously, as having particular substance and noteworthiness. This ache within all of us cannot be satisfied outside of a personal connection with our creator, the Almighty God. Within these pages, you will come to identify your own personal worth and contribution to this world. This will ultimately lead you to proactively rest in your worth, no longer striving for significance, but confidently owning and displaying your value as a solution to the world's various problems.

My advice to you is that reading this book may be a threat to your present life-style. However, it may become the most life-changing book you have read this year. Open your heart and receive the rest and significance that you have longed for and dreamed of for too long.

TABLE OF CONTENTS

SECTION 1: DISSATISFIED

Chapter 1 – Sweat 'N Suffering 1

Chapter 2 – Searching for Satisfaction 9

Chapter 3 – Our Subtle Struggle 13

Chapter 4 – The Five Faces of Deflation ... 21

Chapter 5 – Signs & Symptons 28

Chapter 6 – Early Erosion 31

Chapter 7 – Coming Soon 34

SECTION 2: DISCONNECTED

Chapter 8 – The Weed of Weariness 39

Chapter 9 – Snake in the Grass 42

Chapter 10 – Comparison 53

Chapter 11 – Conformity 59

Chapter 12 – Consumption 64

Chapter 13 – Competition 67

Chapter 14 – Compensation 72

Chapter 15 – Pulling the Plug 76

SECTION 3: SURGING

Chapter 16 – Plug in to Begin 81

Chapter 17 – Relationship 86

Chapter 18 – (Son)day Morning 93

Chapter 19 – Ready to Receive 101

SECTION 4: SELF (HELP)

Chapter 20 – What a Wonderfull Life 111

Chapter 21 – Creation 120

Chapter 22 – Contribution 127

Chapter 23 – Rested 137

Chapter 24 – A Helping Hand 147

SECTION 1
DISSATISFIED

CHAPTER 1

SWEAT 'N SUFFERING

My shirt was dripping with sweat, my heart was pounding through my chest, and my chin tilted up to the sky as I took long, deep breaths— inhale, exhale. I had just finished another great workout, and I headed as usual to the hot box (a.k.a. sauna) for a little R&R before hitting the showers and heading out.

It was just another day at the gym—or so I thought.

Before I could even close my eyes, an extremely thin and very talkative young lady started a conversation without any introduction or asking me whether I minded. It was as if she *needed* to share her burden.

As she rocked back and forth next to the hot coals, she told me she was attempting to sweat as much as possible because she needed to lose just a few more pounds to reach her goals. As she spoke, she vigorously pinched and pulled at her stomach as if to express her repulsion at the sight of her tiny 22-inch waistline.

Her words took me by surprise. I couldn't imagine why she felt this way. Losing more weight was the last thing she needed to do. By my estimate, she was about 5'6" and couldn't have weighed more than 120 lbs.

She then went on to tell me how she worked in a real estate office where she was a successful agent. She was currently pursuing one last certification and once she got that, she'd finally be able to brag to her family and "feel good" about herself. Those were her exact words. I don't know much about real estate, but my wife has her real estate license, and I know from watching her go through the rigorous process of getting licensed that this woman already had plenty to be proud of.

She went on to share with me the stress she experienced due to pressure from her older sister, who was very successful in her own right and was constantly telling her to be thinner, trendier, and more aggressive in the workplace. Her sister said that would ensure she could keep up with millennials who were her "competition." As the woman continued talking, she began to pull at her hair and described how the stress has gotten so bad that her hair was starting to fall out.

Literally.

Can you relate to any of this?

Watching her behavior and listening to her words broke my heart. She may have thought she was just making small talk by sharing a few situations in her life, but what she really was doing was helping me see what she thought of herself. Her beliefs were choking out her confidence, suffocating her sense of significance, and stealing any satisfaction she could have in herself.

I was witnessing a woman suffering from something with which I also grappled for years (and many others still do). Deflation.

In her mind, everything that made her anything was somewhere out in the future. It was something yet to be achieved and attained. It was something outstanding—something she had to do.

That's deflation, the burdensome belief that my worth is something for which I work and must be earned with an exhausting effort. It's the idea that I'm not going to **be** enough until I **do** enough—and even then, it's going to happen someday in the future, not now.

It's the feeling that my work, my hustle, and my grind is what will get me there, wherever "there" is. Unfortunately, that feeling also says it will take even more to keep me there.

To me, this woman represents a multitude of individuals in our society today, including people I've counseled over the last 10 years. They are people who find it extremely difficult to be satisfied with *Self.*

They are people who on the outside appear to have it all and be **do**ing it all but inside they are striving for more. Not for more stuff but for more *Self.*

3

Self is the part of you that has done nothing. It's the part of you that hasn't proven anything to anyone. It's the part of you that is the person not the pursuit, the human not the hustle, the soul not the striving. *Self* is your existence, the *you* apart your efforts.

What is Enough?

*"What else do I have to **do**?"*

"Ok, I did that, is this enough?"

"Will I finally be enough after I've done this?"

"When is enough, enough?"

I once heard Tony Robbins say, "It doesn't matter how many ways you ask. If it's the wrong question, you'll always get the wrong answer."

Are *you* asking the right questions?

Maybe you're not even conscious of it yet, but you know there's a longing within you. You keep trying to satisfy it on your own—and it's not working.

Are you punishing yourself with personal prerequisites that postpone your being satisfied with the present state of everything, including yourself. Are you secretly suffering from an internal interrogation?

Am I enough—of a father? *No*, not if I haven't...

Am I enough—of a mother? *No*, but I will be as soon as I...

Am I enough—of a person? *No*, not yet, but once I...

The list goes on and on and on, and it seems you're never quite enough, are you? This was true for me.

4

Often, we're looking to the wrong things and wrong people for evidence of whether or not we're enough.

As a husband, many times I'd **do** something I thought was "good," then I'd wait and watch how my wife responded. If her response to what I did wasn't good enough (for me), I thought it meant I wasn't good enough (for her).

As a father, I did the same thing. I'd **do** something for my children, and if they didn't appear satisfied, I thought, how could *I* possibly be satisfied.

See how I was equating everything with my *enough*-ness, internalizing and personalizing it all?

The truth is, the phrase **what is enough** is not only a question but more importantly a statement. I want you to know **what** you are is enough. It's time to lighten your load and discover what really brings you happiness in life is something you've always had in your life. You.

I See You

This book isn't for everybody, but it is for somebody— the somebody who's feeling overworked and overwhelmed from the emotional exhaustion of being overlooked, not by others but by yourself. You are, in essence, overlooking what is here today for what you believe will be here tomorrow.

It's for those of you saying, "I'm tired," "I've done everything I know to **do,**" and "I don't know what else I *can* **do.**" It's for those of you wondering if your efforts will ever be enough and looking at yourselves through eyes of emptiness. You're exhausted from all the effort you're exerting and the hard work you're putting in day after day, only to feel that you're never enough.

I want you to know upfront that this book is not a bunch of speculative theories or hearsay but the result and reality of my *personal* restlessness, redemption, relief, and yes—rest.

As someone who's been both tormented and tired, I write to you out of my own weariness, weeping, and worry. For many years, I secretly struggled to someday be enough— that is, enough in my own eyes. If I have not myself shared in the suffering, how can I sincerely say I see yours? But I do.

The first thing I want you to know is I *see* you. Truly, I see your soul, your search, your struggle, and your suffering. In a world where it's so easy to be overlooked and to overlook ourselves, I believe it's important for you to know that's no longer the case for you.

I want you to know from the bottom of my heart that I know the heaviness of the load you carry and that I want nothing more than to help you lighten it. I know what it means to live with a restless soul on a relentless search and to not find what you're looking for.

Obviously, there are many contributing factors to a person's overall dissatisfaction in life. There are many reasons someone experiences mental and emotional fatigue and is "burned out" on life. The intention of this book is to address one of those reasons, namely the idea that you must **do** enough before you can **be** enough.

My Vow to You

I believe you've come across this book at a time and place in your life where you don't require me to corral or convince you of anything. I believe you simply need to know that **what** you're looking for is available and where to find it.

That said, I want to be extremely clear about a few things.

First, this book is *not* a quick fix.

In my experience, quick fixes break quickly. I'm not into patching things up; now is the time for people to experience real progress, not just the appearance of it.

Nor am I providing another cookie cutter, "one size fits all" success system guaranteeing health, wealth, and prosperity in every area of life. It doesn't contain "3 simple steps to..." or "10 keys to ...," etc. You won't find any "90-day plan" or "fool-proof formula" here. I know we live in a society that specializes in handing out hold-me-overs but that's not this book.

I vow not to play mind games and fill your plate with more "To-Do Lists" or hurdles to overcome; there's no more having to **do** enough before you can **be** enough. The only "how to" you'll find is how to lighten the load you're carrying to make room for what you care about most—your happiness.

The truth is, we were created to experience appreciation, not to earn it. If that sounds a little shocking, get used to it. Throughout this book, I'm going to say what others are afraid to say. I'm going to tell you that you don't need my "secrets for success". The only secret you need to know about is the one you've kept from yourself.

This book is faith-based but universally applicable. In other words, deflation has no bias and happiness is for everyone!

I'll refer to the Bible because faith in God has been a vital part of my experience and has helped me get to where

I am today. The life-changing ideas and insights contained in this book have a source and if I were not to tell you about it, it would be like me telling you I had the most amazing meal the other day but refusing to give you the name of the restaurant. Of course, I wouldn't do that. I want you to enjoy what I have and to dine until your soul is satisfied.

In no way do I desire to force feed you my faith, bore you with religious rhetoric, or offend you with judgments. If God is not a part of your current belief system, that's totally OK. God has not always been a part of my life so I can respect your perspective. I want this book to represent a source of sincere acceptance and authentic appreciation for all of humanity.

I want to provide the world with a "standing offer" of something that is available to anyone when they find themselves thinking less of themselves than they should. Regardless of your faith (or lack thereof), if you're at a place where you feel unfulfilled in life or dissatisfied with yourself, this book was written for you.

CHAPTER 2

SEARCHING FOR SATISFACTION

It wasn't long ago that I was like the woman in the sauna, and I find it interesting that this is where our conversation took place. The fact that we've learned to value sweat over *Self* made the location fitting.

Like her, at one time, I also demanded too much of myself. My commandments far exceeded my capacity, and my burden was too heavy for me to bare. To be completely honest, I've always given myself too much responsibility and asked myself to fulfill too many requirements.

My personal expectations were excessive and extended to distances my eyes could no longer see. I constructed hurdles that were unquestionably too high with legs too short to clear those bars.

To everyone else, I was known as a "go-getter," but I knew I was getting more and more frustrated. I was attempting to go everywhere and **do** everything for everyone, but I could never seem to **be** enough for myself.

The truth is that being disciplined and a hard worker comes easily to me. Regimens, routines, and rituals give me a natural high I can't necessarily explain. I'm just wired that way. A sense of frustration and restlessness, however, is not true to who I am.

I just turned 41, and it wasn't until two years ago that I really began to understand the psychology behind the devastating demands I put on myself. I'm now realizing that in my heart of hearts all I ever wanted was to be satisfied with myself.

Most people confronting this issue will say things like, "I just want to be happy." While there's nothing wrong with wanting to be happy, I find that happiness comes and goes depending on a given situation or outcome. I don't believe it quite captures the magnitude of **what** you're missing. Yet I understand for most of us "to be happy" is a phrase we can relate to, and that is why I decided to use it in the title of this book. But when we look beneath the surface, a true sense of satisfaction with one's Self and the ability to rest in the revelation of one's relevance is **what** our souls are searching for.

We're looking for reasons that show us we are more, not how to **do** more. We all want to be enough, don't we? To see ourselves as a significant part of our society and to know that we matter, that our lives stand for something, that we are respected and important. But more than anything, we want to be significant minus the stress and satisfied minus the struggle.

Does that sound familiar?

What would your life be like if I showed you how you could stop struggling to "live up to expectations," or "get it right," or "come through," or "show up," or "fix it" and still be totally accepting of yourself? And **be** enough.

The Name Game

Over the last 12 years, I've worked out of the regional offices of a large health care conglomerate, and my job frequently has required me to visit various medical centers. I got to know many people in each of the centers, yet there were still times I ran into people who looked familiar but I was unable to recall their names.

One of the purposes of this book is to help you put a name to the face of deflation, which has symptoms that can be expressed in many ways. While most us of can describe how it makes us feel, we don't know what to call it. We just know something's not right.

The problem is we're doing what we want but we're not getting what we want. For example, have you ever worked extremely hard to finish a project then went out to celebrate your accomplishment? You took time to rest after seeing the fruits of your labor.

Unfortunately, deflation allows no room for rest. Deflation has us working our asses off and getting all sorts of results but none of them means the job is done.

Why is this? Because the results aren't what we want. We want what we believe these results will deliver but because they never do, we are never satisfied, and our work is never done. This is how the vicious cycle continues.

Have you ever found yourself working hard towards one thing and, as soon as you finish, you're off looking for the next thing to **do**?

Or, it's gotten so bad that even before you finish the initial task, you're already starting to come up with 10 more tasks? Somehow, we intuitively know the results of what we're working on won't satisfy us.

It's kind of crazy when you really stop and think about it, isn't it?

Are you wondering how I know this? Been there, done that. I've lived this thing, and I want you to know that I'm speaking to you, not at you. This book represents a response to your silent cry, a cry that can be heard only by those who have shed the same tears.

If you're in the streets, I was homeless for two years and got into every form of trouble imaginable for another three years; I can talk *street*. If you're corporate, I've been here for more than 12 years; I can talk *corporate*. If you're in the church, I've belonged to one for 18 years and have been an ordained minister for the last eight; I can talk *church*.

I promise not to put limits on you. All I ask in return is that you understand that I don't have any on me.

CHAPTER 3

OUR SUBTLE STRUGGLE

However you slice it, deflation (defined by Merriam-Webster as a reduction in size, importance, or effectiveness) means a decrease or reduction *in* or *of* something.

I first thought about the concept of deflation a few years ago while preparing to preach at a church in Los Angeles. I wanted to illustrate with a visual aid how we come into the world *in*flated—full of possibilities, potential, and promise. But as if someone poked a little hole in us, we slowly begin to deflate until it feels as if we have nothing left. The outer shell is still there but everything inside has been lost.

As I began, I took out a big red balloon like the one from Stephen King's novel "It" and blew it up to its maximum capacity to represent fullness. Then I held it at the end and said, "This is you and me coming into the world." I went on to share some personal struggles, like the times I was bullied as a child and made to feel I was worthless.

As I shared, I paused and let some of the air out of the balloon. I continued this cycle with a few more stories of hurt and disappointment, and by the end, all the air was gone. At this point, I held the balloon up and said, "This is our insides after deflation gets a hold on us, and we are sucked dry of our essential enthusiasm."

It's important to see and understand that deflation is subtle; it happens over time and flies under the radar. The act of air being let out of our sails is a slooooow process that becomes so natural you never even notice it. Our society is filled with people attempting to do something great rather than accepting themselves as something great.

This is what happens when we adopt the idea that we must **do** enough to **be** enough. Our value in the world becomes a chore, a task, a goal—something that needs to be *proven* rather than something that already exists. All of that God energy you were supposed to be using to express yourself has become effort used to earn yourself.

Striving for something that's already there literally sucks the air out of you.

Systematic Satisfaction

Although I was born in Chicago, I grew up in Toledo, Ohio, a small midwestern town 58 miles from the "Motor City" of Detroit.

Growing up there, I was used to seeing huge automotive factories, and both the Jeep and Daimler Chrysler Plants were within walking distance of my homes over the years. My mother's longtime boyfriend and my father-in-law worked for a company called AP Parts, an automotive parts manufacturer that supplied Ford Motor Co.

Needless to say, I became very familiar with large-scale production, assembly lines, and the various aspects of manufacturing.

Companies like Daimler Chrysler invest millions of dollars and thousands of hours to acquire land, buildings, machinery, permits, insurance, and a workforce, all with the intent of manufacturing a very specific and expected product. To do this, they borrow equity from other businesses, apply for financing, take out loans, go into debt, and "bet the house" on building a successful operation—they're all in.

Once they're finally up and running, assembly operations are laid out across the length of the building. At one end, raw materials enter machinery specially designed to cut, melt, pour, and mold them into a specified shape and size.

Once materials pass through all the necessary components, workers stand at the opposite end of the machine ready to receive the finished product, and move them directly onto a new vehicle or into boxes where they are taped shut and prepared for shipment.

This operation is extremely systematic and extremely dependable. Day in and day out, the process remains the same with the same results. With this sort of approach, production is simplified and companies become extremely confident in their ability to meet consumer demand.

New Demand, Same Supply = Dissatisfaction

What would happen if, after experiencing success, things begin to change? What if the system was no longer sufficient — and its machinery incompatible with the innovations of today — so it couldn't provide what people want?

In other words, I'm saying this: Life is like a factory, and your systems are failing. You're no longer getting enough of what your system is giving. The machine is no longer able to make you happy. You gave it a complete overhaul with new parts and even oiled it up pretty well. It appears to be running fine but for some reason the products are poor.

What can you do? This is the only system you know and you've invested everything you have into it. All your heart and soul has gone into building *this* machinery. It was your dream and you depend on it.

The truth is, the system was never truly satisfying in the first place. As we often do, we were simply tolerating a subpar product. When it's all you've ever known, you get used to it and find ways to make it work. You start to think it'll satisfy you one day, someday.

That is, until what's available is no longer adequate. Something deep inside you says it isn't doing it for you anymore. You don't know what will work but you do know the system doesn't satisfy you.

A System Designed to Grind You Down

In our world...

Our <u>Results</u> will someday supply our <u>Relevance</u>.

Our <u>Productivity</u> will someday supply our <u>Prominence.</u>

Our <u>Success</u> will someday supply our <u>Significance</u>.

Deflation is a self-operated system that is supposed to supply us with the product we demand—satisfaction in *Self* (a sense of personal sufficiency and significance). But it is unable to do so.

Deflation is systematically demanding something of yourself you're not designed to deliver. You're doing something over and over to produce proof of your value.

Deflation Is Self-Dependency

I want to stress the point that no matter the design of the demand, it always will be self-dependent. The demand is ours. The system is ours. We've been handed the tools and we built the house. Each of our systems are designed to help us work our way to personal worth. We're trying to use our efforts to manufacture our meaning in life.

Deflation has no bias; it attacks us all, regardless of age, race, religion, political preference, or economic status. Your friends don't matter nor does the amount of money you have in the bank. It doesn't matter how many degrees you have on the wall or what letters come after your name. Business success and awards don't matter either.

Deflation has no limits. Virtually anything can be or become a system; it looks different for everyone. Systems (the self-imposed workload meant to earn our *enough*-ness) can be dramatic or extremely subtle, and they are just as personalized and paralyzing as the person using it.

As long as your behaviors and actions are motivated by wanting to see your significance, the result will be deflation. (I'll use the term "systems of significance" to refer to this throughout the remainder of the book.)

17

Deflation is silent. It doesn't announce itself before it enters your life. It just walks right up, jumps on your back, and starts to hold on for dear life.

Deflation is secret. You know something's not right but you can't figure it out. You see the symptoms but the source evades you. Not only are the people around you unable to pick up on it, many times you're also completely unaware of it yourself.

Your system can be as socially acceptable and undetectable as the one mentioned by the woman I met in the sauna. To most gym rats, she was "going for it," but the truth is she won't be reaching her destination anytime soon. The goal of weighing 105 pounds, once hit, becomes the goal of 102. The waistline goal of 24 inches, once hit, becomes 22 inches.

Note: This shouldn't be confused with self-improvement. Absolutely, you should pursue improving areas of life that need it. Maybe you're in debt so becoming debt-free is absolutely a worthwhile pursuit. Or, you may need to drop a few extra pounds to be healthier, and that's a great idea.

Deflation isn't hard work in and of itself. Hard work doesn't tire your soul, disappointing results do. Your weariness comes from carrying the weight of *why* you're working.

When you're working hard for the sole goal of accumulating enough "evidence" to prove to yourself or others that you're significant or *enough*, you begin to deflate. It's exhausting work because your strength was not intended to be used this way.

Deflation Is a Belief and Behavior System

The belief is that we must first **do** enough before we can **be** enough.

The behavior is any effort we exert to **be**come enough in our own mind.

The Rest*less* Monster

Rich, poor, good, evil, conservative, liberal, gay, or straight—every category we commonly use to distinguish ourselves and appear superior to one other means nothing to this monster. Without warning or waiting for your permission, deflation bulldozes its way into your life and unapologetically takes over.

For some people, it's extremely obvious, for others, it's hard to discern. Some wear their fatigue on their sleeves while others have learned to hide it very well. Sometimes, their apparent success clouds our vision. Just because a person has a lot or does a lot doesn't necessarily mean they have the one thing they truly desire.

Whatever the case, our internal feelings of disappointment, discouragement, and disillusionment are built in; our deflation is by design.

The systems designed by Self-Dependency produce one product and one product only. Deflation.

We have become a restless people struggling to operate a system that is supposed to produce the one and only "product" we are fundamentally unable to manufacture—namely, satisfaction in *Self*.

Systems are great as long as they're working but what happens when it crashes? What happens when it fails and all the "data" you've stored, backed up, and relied on for so long is, all of a sudden, gone?

The truth is that for many of us, our systems already have begun to fail. They've crashed, and in our heart of hearts, we know things are not working anymore.

The problem is, all we know how to do is reboot and try the same things again. We've been taught our entire lives that the only solution to not having what you want in this world is to work harder for it. The message we hear: exert more energy and exercise more willpower.

However you frame it, we've been conditioned to believe if we want more of something, including ourselves, we must **do** more to get it.

The Surprising Thing About Stress

> *"According to the American Psychological Association, chronic stress is linked to the six leading causes of death: heart disease, cancer, lung ailments, accidents, cirrhosis of the liver and suicide. And more than 75 percent of all physician office visits are for stress-related ailments and complaints."*

~ The Miami Herald, March 21, 2014

It's no secret, stress is a killer.

Stress, in whatever form, is the result of "load." Load can be represented in many ways—a physical load as in the weight of a box placed in the back of your pickup truck, or the emotional heaviness you feel when you've been deeply hurt or disappointed.

Several years ago, after losing more than 75 pounds with the help of my close friend, Tony Johnson, I adopted a healthy lifestyle and eventually was inspired to become a Certified Personal Trainer. As a trainer, "load" was introduced to me as a positive concept, a "good stressor."

In the fitness industry, we're taught to use stress to our advantage and growth because the muscles in our bodies will remain the same size and same strength unless they undergo a little stress. By lifting weights or running for long distances, you can consciously control the load. The amount of stress experienced by your body results in your muscles adapting and growing to accommodate it.

It's what happened, for instance, to your childhood friend who now looks like the Incredible Hulk. Stress like that is great for the gym but not so much for your soul.

Deflation Stresses Your Soul

Many people are stressing themselves with what I call "obligation overload." These aren't things we *have* to do, they're things we *believe* we must do. Too many obligations mean too much load and too much load means too much stress. The stressed soul is a soul weakened by the emotional overload of self-imposed deadlines and demands that are too much for us to continue carrying.

It's hard to keep up at this pace. What was once a pleasure has now become a pain. In the rat race, we all will crash and burn at some point, it's inevitable. We can exert only so much effort before we're empty.

Isn't it ironic that the very things we're doing to accumulate everything we believe we need are literally draining us of everything we already have?

CHAPTER 4

THE FIVE FACES OF DEFLATION

1| Deflation Is *Self*-Disappointment

"If it's going to be, it's up to me," we say. This is the original recipe for disaster. No man is an island, and the concept of "self-made" is absolutely absurd. It's a belief that knocks the air out of us and causes us to experience a continual letdown in life.

This demand is suffocating and puts a stranglehold on our satisfaction. We are swamped with ideals and smothered by intentions that we feel must be met in order to prove our place in this world.

As a result, our results are disheartening because they never appear to be enough. It's like we're set up to fail and disappoint ourselves before we ever try.

You end up saying, "I'm an idiot," or "I'll never get this right," or "I hate myself," "What's wrong with me?" or "Here we go again."

Does that sound familiar?

Because your demands are never met, it feels like you keep coming up short every time you measure yourself. You beat yourself down when you don't live up to your own unforgiving standards.

2| Deflation Is *Self*-Depression

When we believe we need to **do** more to **be** more, we literally push ourselves down into a lower position than the one we've been created to occupy. For example, when most of us think of a person plucking a piece of fruit from a tree, we usually get an image of them reaching *up* and pulling it *down*, right?

However, the more I think about what happened in the Garden of Eden (which we'll explore in a little more depth later), the more I imagine they actually reached down for the fruit and pulled *up*. I'm not saying this was literally the case; I am using my imagination, yet I believe there's some validity to it.

(By the way, you'll definitely need to use your imagination a bit to get through the rest of this book.)

The tree was created as something beneath us. In fact, the Bible says we were created a little lower than God, Himself. This means our position on earth is the highest among all living things. Animals and plants, while valuable, were created to assume a *lesser* position than you and me. We were given power over the natural resources of life and yet humans found themselves often succumbing to them.

Anytime we believe that something material will make us better, we're deflated. We think we need a bigger house, better car, nicer clothes, or shinier jewelry. But if these things are in a position to make you feel great about yourself when you have them, they'll make you feel the opposite when you don't.

We have to ask ourselves, what position are we operating from?

3| Deflation Is *Self*-Detainment

Our criminal systems aren't the only ones with a "three-strike" rule. Like a judge in a courtroom, we summon ourselves before the jury of self-judgment. If found guilty, as is usually the case, we sentence ourselves to hours, days, and even years to an internal imprisonment for not living up to our own self-imposed ideals.

Does redemption even exist in our society?

You err or do wrong and society smacks a demoralizing label on you that describes what you've done, and as far as we're concerned, defines **what** you are. Your character is crushed; your soul is slaughtered. Once in the system, when you commit the third strike, the penalty is "to hell with you," and you're thrown away—never to return.

Sadly, this type of sentencing doesn't end with society but continues with Self.

Just imagine how many times you've prevented yourself from moving forward or not allowed yourself to enjoy something or receive love or gifts from others because you didn't believe you were worthy.

Like a judge that sets the bail too high for the defendant to possibly pay or hands down a punishment that doesn't fit the crime, we judge ourselves by marks we're guaranteed to miss.

Even years after failures, we remain in a state of guilt, shame, and condemnation. It doesn't matter what people say, even if they have forgiven you, because your finger is permanently pressed on the instant replay button. In that way, we are detained, and our satisfaction is denied.

4| Deflation Is *Self*-Determination

Who are you to think so little of yourself? I mean really, where did you get the audacity to decide you're so small while other others are so big? Where are your facts? Where's your evidence? What criteria or measurements are you using to determine you're not enough?

Self-determination is like seeing ourselves as glasses half full and thinking we're the only ones who can fill the other half. The funny thing is, if God didn't need our help creating us, why do we believe He needs our help completing us?

In fact, who ever said you were missing something? Who ever said you were incomplete? And if by chance someone actually did tell you this, who the hell are they? Did they create you? Did they give you life? Even our own parents, as much as we may love them and they love us, ultimately, did not make you. Though we came through them, we came from something much greater, the source of our significance. He and He alone gets to determine your value, and the fact that you're here means He already has!

Until we accept this, we'll continue to carry the load of determining our value and wearing ourselves out to prove our importance in society.

5| Deflation Is *Self*-Distortion

A distorted Self is a dissatisfied Self.

I remember a few years back when we could buy those cheap 10 dollar mirrors for the back of your door or to lean against the wall. Without fail, we'd find a way to knock it over, and it would splinter into a million pieces. The good thing about these mirrors was that they were glued to a cardboard frame so none of the glass actually fell out.

When this would happen, I'd pick up the mirror and look at myself for a moment. Sometimes, I'd just catch a glimpse of myself as I lifted it up. Other times, I was more intentional.

What I saw was my reflection in dozens of little fragmented pieces. It was no longer whole, and my image was no longer complete. It looked as though I was full of cracks...or was I?

Deflation is seeing yourself as anything other than enough, anything other than whole. Its only seeing cracks when the thing itself (what is being reflected) is still very much whole.

I didn't change but the mirror did. It had the cracks, not me. What this shows us is that our reflections are only as accurate as the sources we rely on.

Our beliefs are like mirrors, reflecting and projecting images for the soul to see. As long as we believe we must **do** enough to **be** enough, we'll never see images that reflect enough. Consequently, our soul is never satisfied with what it sees and is unable to rest until it does.

The Deflated Soul

The deflated soul is the weary and burdened soul, depleted like a balloon with a tiny hole in it and air seeping out slowly but steadily.

The deflated soul is the soul that demands much more than it can possible do. It is living with full hands but an empty heart.

The deflated soul is an overworked and overwhelmed soul that refuses to rest, and believes just a little more effort and that'll be enough. Our soul screams out for rest but our struggle says no.

Question: What kind of runner finishes a marathon and before even looking at the medal around his neck walks back over to the starting block and lines up again?

Answer: The deflated one. The one who is stuck where he starts because it's never enough.

As with many of our behaviors, we're unable to explain with a sense of confidence why we do them. Deflation is no different.

The truth is, deflation has been developing since we were born. We're inundated with ideas and images that direct our ambitions away from what we already *are* to what we *are to become*.

From the time we're old enough to understand, society bombards us with messages, and our minds begin constructing the futuristic framework around which we build our lives.

Heeding the call of tomorrow, we neglect today.

27

CHAPTER 5

SIGNS & SYMPTOMS

Just as having a weak immune system makes it more likely for us to catch colds, being born into a bad belief system predisposes us to deflation. In most cases, this occurs because our parents and/or those most influential in our earliest stages of life were themselves deflated, and they unknowingly "infected" us with their poor thinking.

It's important to note that deflation occurs on a subconscious level. Most of us are so busy we never slow down long enough to really contemplate the root cause of our restlessness, so we continue to put out fires with the sweat dripping from our foreheads.

The symptoms are recognizable (I'm not happy, I'm tired, I'm stressed, etc.) so we address them with our best effort. Nevertheless, the damaging source of our woes is never remedied.

Worth-*less*

At a very early age, I began to experience things that terrified me and tore to shreds any confidence I had in myself as a person.

Physical, emotional, mental, and spiritual abuse, some of which I share in detail later in the book, brought me to a place where I was willing to die for $120.

I was around 19 years old and had just purchased an ounce of marijuana for $120 from some guys with whom I had no business dealing. This was common in the "hood." Money was what mattered so even if they didn't like *you*, your money was always good.

After the transaction, I was offered a ride home and figured it was no big deal. We had just done business, I thought, *whatever*. But as we approached my neighborhood, the driver said he needed to urinate, and he pulled into a nearby alley. As soon as he got out, two guys with their faces covered in purple bandanas ran up to the car. One of them pulled out a gun and pointed it at my head through the open window.

With the muzzle of his gun pressed against my left temple, he began to scream, "Give me the shit, give me the weed, give me your money!"

I begin to push the marijuana down my pants, saying, "No, I don't have it."

This was obviously a setup because how could he possibly have known I had anything to begin with? I'm just a guy sitting in the back seat of a car. By saying no, I was refusing to give it to him versus pretending I didn't actually have it. In other words, I was willing to die for $120. He knew I had it. I knew I had it. But the threat of being shot in the head and dying wasn't enough for me to let go.

After a few moments of this back and forth, he pulled the trigger. I heard the gun's hammer go *POP*, but nothing happened.

Whenever I share this story on stage, I always emphasize this particular moment because a man with an empty gun doesn't pull the trigger. I believe it wasn't empty. He tried to kill me that day, and if it hadn't been for a miracle, he would have succeeded.

I believe God spared my life by preventing the bullet from being fired. My life, for whatever reason, was meant to continue on, and thank God it did.

The gunman ran off, and I was left to run home on my own. As I ran, I remember being so proud of myself, I yelled, "Yeah, I didn't give up shit. That nigga ain't get shit from me."

As I look back now, my heart breaks. He didn't "get shit from me" because I felt like life had already taken everything. In my mind, I was worthless so the weed had more value than my life. I had no dreams or confidence for the future. I was deflated enough to die for $120.

I share this story because I believe it represents a million other untold stories around the world. They are stories of lives devastated by deflation and some of those lives, unlike mine, were not spared.

CHAPTER 6

EARLY EROSION

As a father of four amazing children, I've become very familiar with childbirth. Obviously, I'm not nearly as familiar with it as my wife but I'd like to think I've been an equal participant. (Female readers, I understand if you are rolling your eyes right about now, *LOL*.)

My point is, I was front and center for every appointment and ultrasound as well as the days each of my children came into the world.

When a child is born, the doctor announces its gender, and the parents are filled with love and admiration. The baby's very arrival is appreciated and electrifying. The parents hug, kiss, and embrace their child and begin taking pictures to share with the world.

What's both amazing and agonizing about this moment is that birth is usually the only moment in our lives when we're considered enough for everyone without our needing to meet their expectations.

Fast forward a few years >>>

"What do you want to **be** when you grow up?" Does that sound familiar? Can you recall the person who asked you? Or at what age they popped the big question?

Society wastes no time bombarding us with the burden of (**be**)coming. Although we're born free of shame and self-judgment, society soon swoops in on us and before we know it, we're looking at ourselves sideways with no true sense of our inherent value.

We're asked this question for a million reasons.

Some people want to know our desired occupations to encourage us to pursue our dreams. Others want to know so they can tell us the best specific course of action to ensure our success.

Obviously, I could provide more examples, and whoever is asking this question usually has good intentions. That's not the problem. The problem is what the question implies and how it may impact our lives.

Our overworked and overwhelmed lives can be traced back to infancy. Before we ever get a chance to see **what** we already are, we're taught to paint our pictures of "tomorrow" rather than admiring our portraits of today.

The implications are subtle but significant. Without even realizing it, we're suddenly sucked into the rest-*less* world of "When I…," "One day I'll…," and "As soon as I…."

This popular question represents a larger group of questions, slogans, sayings, and clichés that are so prevalent in our society that they have come to be "just a part of life," as misguided as they are. Anxiety and anticipation have become de facto parts of our psyches.

We're such a dissatisfied society because we're such an impatient one. Impatience is directly connected to anticipated results. You're only impatient because you want to get somewhere. I believe the same is true of our relationship with our Self.

We judge, degrade, devalue, and of course, deflate the present Self because we never seem to get where or what we believe will make us enough fast enough.

Reality's rushed pace is regarded as a rite of passage so our beliefs and behaviors appear to be natural. We've been **do**ing this our entire lives. Aren't we supposed to be ahead of the curve?

Could this be why we have such little regard not only for ourselves but also for one another? Or why our society is suffocating itself with superficial priorities?

Inner beauty takes time to see and appreciate (sitting, listening, honoring), which we never seem to have as we *zoom-zoom-zoom* to our next "important" destination.

From a very young age, how we see or, more importantly, don't see ourselves is heavily influenced by a future-focused society. Deflation is opportunistic and at our most impressionable ages, we're taught to "shoot for the moon" as if there's not enough on Earth to explore.

CHAPTER 7

COMING SOON

*"You can be so into the possibilities of tomorrow
that you miss the pleasures of today.*

— Bishop T.D. Jakes

Everywhere we go, future is the focus. Rarely are we satisfied with the present state of anything.

In the 20 years my wife and I have been together, we've been blessed to have four amazing children. Being a family of six means juggling six personalities and preferences. With this diversity, finding common ground and things we all can enjoy simultaneously is of great importance.

34

Over the years, we've discovered several family activities, but one comes to mind as I think about the topic of this book—movies. Whether its loading up the car and heading out to the theater, stopping off at a Redbox on the way home, or simply ordering something on the television, we really enjoy watching movies even if it means we must deal with the previews.

Over the last few years, I've noticed a substantial increase in the number of previews. Have you? Back in my day (and I may be dating myself here), we *maybe* saw one or two previews. As I got older, it was more like three or four. Recently at the movies, and I'm not exaggerating, my family and I sat through 20 minutes' worth of previews. That's right—20 minutes. We even timed it.

I mean, don't get me wrong, they were exciting and each preview brought more intrigue. We saw captivating cliffhangers and heard dramatic music that stirred our emotions as the words COMING SOON scrolled across the cinema screen.

This combination of theatrical temptations never fails to leave you saying, "I can't wait till that comes out! I gotta see that as soon as it comes out. That's going to be awesome!"

Sound like anything you've said?

Sadly, many of us are living our lives this way. Going through life is like going to the movies. We want to see what's already finished and ready for viewing. But instead, we're sidetracked with the upcoming attractions.

Do you ever find yourself stuck, staring at the exciting previews rather enjoying the actual feature?

Essentially, we're taught to forfeit today's satisfaction for a forecast of tomorrow's sights and sounds. Let me ask you, have you ever considered that today is yesterday's tomorrow?

The Future Freaks

From infancy, we've been inundated and, in many ways, intimidated into adopting a futuristic focus. I'm serious. We've become a bunch of future freaks.

Think about it: Where can you go and whom can you talk to when the conversation isn't about something down the line? It's always what we are about to do, where we are about to go, what we are about to get, and what's about to happen.

I mean I understand that planning for the future is responsible, and seeing beyond your current circumstances is critical. But so is beholding the beauty of your *now*. It's OK to anticipate tomorrow as long as you appreciate today.

You've heard the saying, "Stop and smell the roses." In this fast-paced, future-minded society, rarely are we allowed to slow down enough to do that. How tragic when you learn that you're the rose and the scent of *Self* is what you've been passing up all these years.

The Wait, The Truth, and The Life

Such intense inundation has created a future frenzy that's beginning to infiltrate even the one place where you'd think we could take refuge. Sunday morning used to be a day of rest, and the church was a place we could recover and regroup before heading back out into the weekday whirlwind. Not anymore.

The future has forced its way into American church culture and taken a front row seat. "God's *about to* do something amazing in your life," or "Get ready, God's *about to* show up," or "Just keep holding on child of God, your breakthrough is *on its waaaaay.*" I guess God is a future freak, too.

Of course, as an ordained pastor myself, I understand the heart of these messages, and in no way am I recommending we throw the baby out with the bath water. I get why we say what we say, yet I fear that by overselling the future, we're overlooking the present. We're preaching future-day abundance while the souls of people are starving for present-day adequacy.

With such extreme emphasis on the future state of everything, is it any wonder that we're so dissatisfied with the current state of anything, including *Self?*

Tomorrow is the greatest enemy of today.

SECTION 2
DISCONNECTED

CHAPTER 8

THE WEED OF WEARINESS

By definition, a weed is known as "a plant in the wrong place," according to Nikki Tilley, author of *The Bulb-o-licious Garden*.

She writes, "For the most part, these plants are known more for their undesirable qualities rather than for their good ones, if there are any. Weeds are competitive, fighting your garden plants or lawn grass for water, light, nutrients, and space. Most are quick growers and will take over many of the areas in which you find them. While most types of weeds thrive in favorable conditions, native types may be found growing nearly anywhere the ground has been disturbed." (Phipps, Nikki, 2010).

Weeds of weariness, as I call them, can and will grow as natural ones do—anywhere. They literally fight for the very things your "flower" should be getting. A flower is **what** God has created you and me to **be** so we can flourish in the garden we call life.

What we should be getting is all the water, light, sun, nutrients, and space in our lives, yet we have weeds fighting for those resources and, in many cases, winning. Weeds are the systems we've set up to earn our ability to be enough. Our systems continue to edge out *Self* and swallow all the nutrients that rightfully belong to us.

Weeds clutter and complicate our gardens. The beauty is still there; weeds just make it harder to *see*. This is an important point to understand—just because we're not able to see something at the present moment doesn't mean it's not there. Just because you can't see yourself being enough right now doesn't mean you're not.

Like the weeds growing in our gardens, deflation grows wild throughout the landscape of our lives, creating cultural chokeholds and causing many of us to tap out long before *we* ever get a chance to flourish.

Those of us suffering from deflation are well acquainted with the self-suffocating squeeze these weeds have on our lives. Whether we feel we're never *good* enough, never *have* enough, or never can *do* enough, in the end its about *enough*. If we want to pull up these "weeds," we must start at the root where the seed was sown.

Seed of Sabotage

Everything has an origin or starting point, a seed from which life springs and grows. Do you have an apple tree in the backyard? It started with an apple seed. Are you expecting a new baby? He or she began with egg and sperm seeds. Opening a new business? It started with the seed of an idea. If it exists, it started with a seed, and deflation is no different.

Once I began to notice the effects of deflation and researched how it worked (what it was doing to me and to others), I came across a passage in the Bible that's given me the best insight into its origins.

In the pages to follow, I want to offer to you what I learned and how I see it. This is not a Bible study but a *burden* study examining how I began to cross reference ideas with my life experiences and made sense of it all.

This process opened my eyes to things I had not previously seen in myself or society as a whole, and I became convinced they were universal in their impact. I saw many people going through similar experiences and thought my newly acquired knowledge could help them.

A few years ago, my close friend, financial advisor, and personal mentor, Rusty Proctor, took me under his wing and coached me on communication.

"If you say it, they'll tend to doubt it," he told me. "If they say it, they'll believe it."

I will not attempt to force feed you evidence to support my personal view, like some self-help books. No, my intention is to simply share the following information in a way that's relevant and easy to digest while leaving plenty of room for your brilliance, creativity, and genius to cultivate convictions that fit your life and best serve you on your journey.

CHAPTER 9

SNAKE IN THE GRASS

I'm going to be completely honest with you: Some things in life we can't explain, don't understand, and may never know, but this is no reason for us to not make the best decisions we can with the available information. I say this because I can't tell you why the serpent had a beef with our Creator, but what I do know is that he thought the best way to hurt Him was to hurt *us*.

The Approach

The Bible says the serpent was crafty. In other words, the snake knows what he's doing. He's not an amateur. Anyone can tell a lie, but not everyone is skilled in the art of deception, which is what we're discussing.

1 Now the serpent was more crafty [subtle, skilled in deceit] than any beast of the field which the Lord God had made. And he said to the woman, "Indeed, has God said, 'You shall not eat from any tree of the garden'?" 2 The woman said to the serpent, "From the fruit of the trees of the garden we may eat; 3 but from the fruit of the tree which is in the middle of the garden, God has said, 'You shall not eat from it or touch it, or you will die.'"

Did you notice the serpent's approach? The serpent came out the gate with a question, not an accusation, which came later. Doesn't that strike you as odd? I remember times in my life when someone was lying to me, and they approached me with something like, "Man, let me tell you what so-and-so did."

The point is, they couldn't wait to just flat-out tell me what I "needed" to know. But not the serpent, he needed to set the stage. See, the fact is you are enough—always have been, always will be—period, end of story. But what good are facts if they aren't what you're looking at? And you don't believe them?

Direct (Quest)ions

As a public speaker and professional communicator, one of the first things I was taught was to open my speech or presentation with a compelling and direct question. Why? Questions direct our focus—in other words, our mental *quest*.

Our energy—including our thoughts, ideas, imagination, critical thinking, and problem-solving abilities—are fully engaged when a question is asked of us. What we focus on becomes bigger, and the bigger the object, the larger the quest. Questions are profound in this way. They cause us to search for personal conclusions and create personal convictions. This goes back to my point about Rusty's advice, which was to allow people to say it for themselves so they believe it.

The serpent knew he wanted to direct our behavior and make us eat from the tree. So instead of simply telling us to eat, he led us in developing the *belief* that we needed to.

Our minds are mini problem-solvers. Questions stimulate the mind and suggest we need to take action and produce a solution. Our solutions become our opinions and, if left unattended and unaddressed, will ultimately lead to a belief.

Belief is perhaps the most influential and impactful resource we possess because it dictates behavior. People don't do what they know, they do what they believe.

"Beliefs are nothing more than feelings of certainty about what something means."

— Tony Robbins

This is more than being told a lie and believing it. This is about your being deceived into making the lie your truth and allowing it to guide your actions and behaviors. This is where we are as a society; the lie is now our truth. We've taken full responsibility for the idea that we're not enough and if we will just **do** more, someday we will **be** enough.

This idea of deception and stage-setting reminds me of society's love for magic acts. Much like the serpent, magicians use similar strategies to amaze and trick their audiences.

The Illusion

As one who grew up loving magic and watching illusionists perform on TV for years, I learned early on that the foundation of any trick is what I call The Swap of State.

By "state," I mean the aesthetic attributes of a given object or person, including condition, type, shape, size, color, amount, etc. Every trick or illusion has a beginning state and ending state; it's all about changing or *swapping* the state without being caught.

In order to pull this off, the illusionist must master the craft of deception—the ability to redirect our focus long enough to make us begin to see what isn't as if it is and what is as if it isn't.

Sound Familiar?

I'm sure we've all seen the one where a woman is placed in the glass box, a large sheet is thrown over it, the magician snaps their finger, the sheet is pulled away, and wham! The woman has become a tiger. Or when the magician shows us his empty hand, tightens it into a fist, and waves a wand over it. When he opens his hand, a big beautiful bouquet of flowers suddenly appears.

Whatever the case, while we're watching in amazement what we believe to be the trick, the magician or illusionist understands the real magic is in redirecting our focus and mental energy away from the swap—the point at which they exchange one thing for another.

And so it is with us.

Originally, our attention was on what we already were, had and could do; our sense of insufficiency or being "not enough" did not yet exist, and our self-portrait was pristine.

But a successful career as an illusionist depends on the ability to deceive you. They must be able to hold your attention and redirect your focus from what's really happening.

I recall a perfect example from a TV special called "Street Magic" featuring my favorite illusionist, David Blaine. He was performing random tricks with strangers as he walked around New York City. After performing several successful tricks, he performed one that reminded me of the serpent and his deception.

It was the middle of the day, and he approached a woman standing in a crowd of at least 20 people. Even with witnesses, Blaine took the woman's watch off her wrist without anyone noticing.

First, he asked her name and if she was willing to participate. After she agreed, he handed her two playing cards and told her to keep her eyes on them. He then loosely held both of her wrists while moving her hands in a back-and-forth motion while instructing her again to keep watching the cards in her hands.

She obviously was under the impression that the trick was about the cards because all of her focus was on anticipating what would happen with the cards. Yet nothing could have been further from the truth.

The entire time, Blaine intentionally kept her engaged with conversation. Everything he said came off as being very casual and unassuming—innocent, even. Little did she know just how impactful the conversation would turn out to be. It wasn't the cards or even the fact he was holding her hands the whole time that made the trick work. It was what he was *saying* and getting *her to say* that sealed the deal.

46

You know, it's hard to focus on several things at once. It doesn't work all that well, does it? Something is going to get overlooked. She was so locked in on the conversation while still trying to focus on the cards, he was able to steal her watch in broad daylight. As they say, he robbed her blind.

I use this well-known term to make a point. Obviously, she wasn't literally blind; she stared at the cards in her hand during the trick. Blind in this context and the context of our lives means loss of (*in*)sight, as in mental and even spiritual awareness. Awareness, consciousness, perception, and understanding are all forms of *in*sight.

Do you see where we're going with this? Sure, her eyes were open but her awareness was closed for business.

After two minutes of talking, waving her hands, and staring at cards, the wait was over. Blaine let go of the woman's wrists and asked a few more questions. You've got to build the suspense, right? Then, all of sudden, she began to look puzzled. What she anticipated never happened— nothing about the *cards* ever changed—yet something about *her* did.

Rather than allow her to suffer any longer, David smiled, reached in his pocket and pulled out her wristwatch. At first, she seemed even more confused. It belonged to her but she didn't recognize it at first (think about that!). After a few more seconds of silence, it came to her and her hand flew up to her mouth as she cried out, "Oh my God, that's my watch."

Could it be that we, too, were so locked in on the conversation with the serpent and our focus so misdirected that we became *blind* to what was really happening to us?

The serpent said to the woman, "You surely will not die. For God knows that in the day you eat from it your eyes will be opened, and you will be like God, knowing good and evil."

There's a whole lot of conversation happening. Do you think we were losing a little focus and our awareness was growing a little dull?

Do you think we're starting to see God in a new light? Is God starting to look a little suspect now? Is God holding back on us?

It's my belief that in this moment the Seed of Dissension (with our Source) was sown. Are you starting to think about this whole God and tree thing a little differently?

Well, God told us *not* to eat from it; he never said we *couldn't*. And besides, if He's holding back on us, can He be trusted anymore? I mean it's right there, maybe we should just *get it ourselves* since He's not giving it to us.

It's my belief that in this moment the Seed of Dependency (on our Self) was sown. Can you see the wheels turning?

Wait you mean we're not like Him, but we can be if we take action? You mean there's something missing in us, but we can recover it if we just do this? We're not complete? We need more? We're not enough now?

These are all possible questions racing through our minds now, questions that never occurred to us before. And at this point, the answer to them all is what we will do!

Remember, the mind is a solution-seeking machine so it's very possible our minds were working overtime thinking of ways we could solve the problem: OK, if God is holding back on us, and if what we lack is just an arm's reach away, why not just do it ourselves?

It's my belief that in this moment the Seed of Deficiency (in our Self) was sown.

The Reach

The tool was our hand, but the target was our head. When all of our attention and focus is on not having enough, we focus on our ability to make up for it. We're ready for action.

Let's take another look at David Blaine's deception.

I pointed out that he held the woman's wrists to move them back and forth. What I didn't explain is that he didn't do so forcefully; it was more like guidance than force.

The grip was so unassertive that she began to make the motion on her own after a while. She was so focused on the cards that his grip was secondary, soon becoming less and less noticeable. She was totally consumed. The problem is, as the story goes, so were we.

Biting Off More Than We Could Chew

> When the woman saw that the tree was good for food, and that it was a delight to the eyes, and that the tree was desirable to make one wise, she took from its fruit and ate; and she gave also to her husband with her, and he ate.

The serpent no longer needed to "hold our hands" as we do with someone who lacks confidence in what they're doing. No, our minds were made up, and we thought we knew what we wanted and how to get it, so we reached.

This was a brilliant tactic as it not only untied the knot of our own balloon, as it were, but it also encouraged us to open the valve and take up the work of deflating ourselves.

I call this moment "the reach" for several reasons. The first is that we literally needed to reach out and pull from the tree in order to eat from it. The second reason is not as obvious. I believe this reach was the first of many and is the foundation of our frustration today. To me, it was the inaugural System of Significance and the blueprint for "If I **do** enough, I'll **be** enough."

We lacked something internal (wisdom, knowledge, etc.) so we attempted to gain it by something external (strife, work, efforts, toil, struggle, etc.). We extended our physical arm for the attainment of a spiritual attribute. It's extremely important to understand that what the body does outwardly is first done inwardly. In other words, our external direction is the result of our internal directives.

I believe this episode laid the foundation for today's pursuit of perfection, prosperity, and prominence. The effort to become enough started then and continues today.

When the woman reached for the "fruit," not only did her hand extend but so did her heart; in fact, her heart reached first. Not only was this an act of self-reliance but of rebellion. Until this point, we relied on our Creator, our God, our Source, for everything. When we were deceived into believing we needed to take matters in our own hands, we essentially said, "We no longer need you; we got this."

The Swap

Just as the woman unknowingly swapped her watch for two worthless playing cards, I believe we swapped our precious perception of *being* enough for the pursuit of *becoming* enough. For what? The Swap of State.

Everything David did—from the conversation and the cards to the questions and handholding—was all for the moment he could successfully swap the state of the woman's watch from her wrist to his pocket. Once this was done, his mission was complete.

The moment we acted, our state was swapped. By believing we needed to **do** something before we could **be** something, our pleasure became a pain and our delight became a demand. What was once easy for us to see became nearly impossible to recognize.

Then the eyes of both of them were opened, and they knew that they were naked; and they sewed fig leaves together and made themselves loin coverings.

Isn't this interesting?

All of a sudden, we find ourselves feeling compelled to do things for ourselves we've never done before. We have concerns we've never had and work in ways we never did.

And so it is today. Just as a history of cancer runs through a family's genealogy, predisposing bloodlines to disease, so does their reach now render us susceptible to the systems of deflation.

Ever wonder about the concept of "the fall" of man in Genesis? Could it be because it was in this moment that we first attempted to support ourselves, and we were unable to?

At least that's how I see it.

"The secret of contentment is knowing how to enjoy what you have and to be able to lose all desire for things beyond your reach."
— The Secret of Contentment | William B. Barcley

Criminal Minded

Another way of looking at dissatisfaction is through the eyes of contentment, which is a state of happiness or satisfaction.

There are 50 states in the U.S., none of which are named Contentment. This is a play on words, yes, but no laughing matter. Deflation seems to have become our new domain. Where can you go nowadays and find any significant population truly content, not only with what they have but, most importantly, with **what** they are?

Who stole our satisfaction?

Let me share with you examples from a few of the most criminal systems in our society. Systems that clutter our lives and cloud our judgement, robbing us of our satisfaction. Comparisons, Conformity, Consumption, Competition, and Compensation are the crooks.

My hope is that you won't simply take my word for it but instead conduct a thorough investigation and interrogate each one to see what they may have that rightfully belongs to you. It's restitution time.

CHAPTER 10

COMPARISON

We live in a world of extremes. From extreme makeovers to extreme sports, it's become extremely important to appear extremely important. We go overboard in our attempts to get attention.

When I was a child, my grandma said, "Oh, that boy's just doing that to get attention." Yes, I was, actually. People want attention because they associate attention with appreciation and acceptance, both of which help us feel like we're enough. We get boob jobs, butt jobs, lips jobs, full body tattoos, facial piercings, and I'm sure a few more things I'm not aware of.

I share this not to judge, because I don't. I have tattoos and plan on getting more. I share this because of what doing these things often means. Obviously, that's not to say everyone is begging for attention so they can feel important, but suffice it to say there's enough people who do these things to mention them.

Comparisons cheat us out of our contentment because it doesn't allow us to behold the beauty of life and certainly not appreciate the accomplishments of others without turning it into some sort of personal assessment.

Does this sound like anything you've ever said or at least thought: How the hell can they afford that house already? Damn, I know I make more than them. I've been working my ass off, saving for a down payment, and improving my credit for years, and I still can't buy one yet.

For all you know, someone in their family could have just passed away and left them a trust that was enough to pay off a home or at the very least get them into one. Their situation has nothing to do with yours but you find a way to make it about you.

Besides, the grass may be "greener on the other side" but the water bill's a bitch. Sometimes it's a blessing in disguise you don't have everything you want or think you should.

Babies think, hey, he's got a bottle, I only have a pacifier—I want a bottle.

Kids think, hey, they got the iPhone X, I only have the 6—I want a X.

Adults think, hey, he or she just got a promotion, I'm still in the same position—I want to move up in the company, too.

The luster of our new whatever starts to fade the moment we look up and see what someone else is wearing or driving or where they are living. Wanting valuable things is not wrong, but what's wrong is wanting valuable things because we associate them with *our* value in society.

The designer clothing, high-end cars, and exclusive residences are all subject to change and far too fragile to support your future significance. So why do we compare ourselves to others? Because we believe there's a possibility that we aren't enough.

If you're someone who compares yourself to others, it means your operating your life by what I call "sensory significance." You're basing your value on what you can sense (see, touch, smell, hear, and taste). Unfortunately, the minute your senses go dull (like a person needing new glasses) so does your significance.

Comparisons are never really about what others have but about what you believe you don't. Comparisons are rooted in our own insecurities, and you feel dissatisfied because you think you'll never match up to others. Not because they are so great but because you feel so small. You're so convinced of your lack that others automatically appear to **have** or **be** more.

What's wild about this is that the very people we envy are often looking at us and thinking the same thing. "They" always appear to have "it" better.

Please recognize that I understand. I know where you are, what you're feeling, what you're experiencing. This is not a topic many people discuss or are able to effectively articulate, so something had to be said.

I once thought the same way. It's not easy living in a society saturated with photoshopped models in fashion magazines, flawlessly filtered selfies on social media, and Hollywood stars on every channel.

Wait, did you catch that? *Stars.*

Where did that description come from? And what qualifies celebrities, not us, to be considered stars? Isn't their job acting, singing, and dancing? Don't they go to work, just like you and me? Aren't they paid for their services or skills, the same as us (though maybe at not the same level)?

Why does this hierarchy exist in our society? Why are celebrities mobbed by photographers and waited on hand-and-foot? Yet when you and I walk down those very same streets, no one notices us at all? We're looked over as if we're not even there.

It's this sort of nonsense that invokes unconscious comparisons and entices so many young people to chase dreams of celebrity, even if they have no actual interest or talent in performance or art. The deflated soul is desperate for the validation that these professions appear to provide—namely, greater status in the system.

The problem with this system is that it's not so much what it says about the other person as much as what we believe it says about us by comparison. If they're "stars," you ask, then what am I?

Deflation is a gut-wrenching reality for so many of us. We see value everywhere except the one place it matters most—in ourselves. We're able to see a reflection of relevance in everyone else, but when the mirror of life is held up to our faces, it's as if nothing is there.

For me, the struggle started in elementary school when I began to gain weight and my stuttering became more apparent in and out of class. I'd often compare myself to others and wonder why I wasn't skinny like the other boys or why I couldn't talk without an impediment. The kids picked on me and made fun of me, so I began to see myself as a joke, as someone undeserving of acceptance.

I don't know what deep-rooted pain you've had to endure but the truth is we're all struggling with something. We all have shortcomings, and comparing ourselves to others never helps us to shift our attitude and feel that we are enough.

"You can't be what you can't see."

— Bishop T.D. Jakes

In my early years in ministry, many people told me that I'd be a pastor and have a church one day. No matter how many times I heard this, I could not see becoming a pastor myself.

But when Eric said I was a teacher, that instantly felt right. I could handle that, and accepting it was very exciting and gave me a sense of purpose. I love to talk, and I love to teach and show people how to do just about anything. So yeah, teacher—yup, got it.

But pastoring, I just couldn't *see* it.

At the time, I didn't realize what was obstructing my view were all the comparisons I made about myself in relation to others. Things began to change when I had a conversation with a close friend and mentor, Dr. Dwayne Cantrell, Pastor of Living Victory Church in Bakersfield, CA.

57

Dwayne was a pastor on our staff at the time, and when I told him how I didn't see myself in that light, he showed me something new. He shared with me the idea that being a pastor did not look a certain way. I didn't have to fit into a mold or do things the way others did. He showed me I could be a pastor and still be myself.

I recall his words like it was yesterday.

"Being a pastor is being a shepherd, and shepherding has no template," he said.

He taught me that how you shepherd, how you love people, and how you care for the soul of humanity is as unique as you are.

For the first time, I could begin to see myself as a pastor. I even began recognizing that I had been doing it all along, but I had been blinded by comparisons. After a year of consideration and fasting for 21 days, I felt in my heart it was time and that God was choosing me to help shepherd his people.

What started with a conversation ended with a confirmation: I was a pastor. To this day, I tell that story to young men I mentor to help encourage them to see new ideas about themselves. To do for others what Dwayne did for me.

Had Dwayne never helped me look past my comparisons, I never would have believed I could do what now completely captivates me. Dwayne, whom I respect and admire, showed me that pastoring wasn't something I had to become but something I *already* was.

Thanks, Dr. D.

CHAPTER 11

CONFORMITY

We were born inspired, creative, energetic, and full of life. But early on, society pokes tiny holes in our balloons. You know the ones, the kind you make when you want to let the air out really slowly, just small enough to not be noticed and big enough to be effective. We've been deflating for so long that it's nearly impossible to see ourselves as being any different, as inflated and constantly rising to new heights.

Conformity Is the New Normal

Being discouraged, disillusioned, and disheartened should be a red flag, a signal telling us that something is wrong. But this soul struggle has so woven itself so deeply into the fabric of our society that it's become normal. But is it, really?

Remember, we're bombarded with questions as children and never get a chance to make an accurate assessment of ourselves. Many of our parents had no idea of their own significance so how could they have possibly given us any idea of ours? Soon after we're born, we're crammed into the classroom of conformity where we learn to accept a predefined Self and a cookie-cutter Self—a mold for the masses.

Self-Dependency is the subject, people, and we're all given a crash course. It's this "one size fits all" approach that suppresses the human soul and deflates the unique brilliance each of us brings into this world.

We're restless, sleepless, and just flat-out tired. The world screams, "Get your ass in gear, that's no longer in fashion, that's not in season, that's not trending—KEEP UP, STAY UP, and GET ON BOARD. Conform to our ways or just get out of our way."

TV commercial says, "You do you," but can you?

I mean, is doing you really doing *you* or is it the you they've conditioned you to be? Sounds confusing huh? Good, that's just how this system wants it.

The less you know about you, the more society can inundate, intimidate, and influence you with messages about how to be like everyone else.

In my research on the concept of conformity, I discovered that there are two primary types: compliance and conversion.

Compliance conformity is the act of conforming only in public while conversion conformity is the act of altering personal beliefs and behaviors to conform both in public and private. Regardless of type, conformity is the result of our less-than-enough estimation of Self.

Although all of the systems we'll discuss are unstable by nature and inadequate to supply our demand, conformity is perhaps the most volatile. When we're consumed with conforming to society's standards, we live like rag dolls.

Let me explain. As a child, I was raised by my grandmother, a part-time registered nurse and full-time master seamstress and dollmaker. A shelf overlooking her sewing machines displayed many of her dolls, and they became conversation pieces among visitors.

One doll, in particular, always sat on the edge of the shelf. It was a little girl with bright red hair, a blue shirt, white dress, and black shoes. My grandmother made the doll by hand and named it "Raggedy Anne" after the classic cartoon character.

Raggedy Anne would get pulled down more than any other doll on the display shelf. The kids would play with her, pulling at her arms and tossing her around. The dog would use her as a chew toy. After a while, we'd find Raggedy Anne on the floor or in another room altogether.

The way we used and abused her made the name seem perfect, and it was as if my grandmother knew the doll's destiny was to be dragged around and beat up until it couldn't sit up on its own anymore. Raggedy Anne would just sort of lean on the shelf, often sliding down to where it looked like it was either taking a nap or dead.

Do you ever go through life feeling like Raggedy Anne, as if life is literally dragging you around by the foot as your head bounces on the ground?

Do you ever feel like your emotions, thoughts, moods, attitudes, and beliefs are all over the place, without any consistency? Do you feel like society's rapid pace means that if you take a day off from conforming, you'll no longer be informed?

I know that feeling. Feeling like I can't keep up with the fast pace pressures of progress, prosperity, and of course, popularity. As soon as you buy that kind of (fill in the blank), it's obsolete. Then as soon as you run and get the new (fill in the blank), it's outdated.

You've been going back and forth in your mind on the crowd's way of doing things for weeks, and as soon as you decide to do it their way, it changes. Have you ever asked yourself, "When did I start caring so damn much about what others were doing, let alone how they were doing it? At what age did I start to believe I needed to be 'in fashion?' When did I become so consumed with clearing all the check points of commonality?"

These are the questions I asked myself and my oldest son while we waited to be seated at a restaurant for a Mother's Day dinner last year. I saw a toddler fumble and stumble around in the lobby. This little guy's shorts were coming down because his diaper was heavy and his socks weren't matching. The point is, he was looking rough and smelly, but he was just as happy as he could be. Bouncing around smiling and enjoying life without a care in the world.

Don't you want to again fumble and stumble happily not caring about what you have or don't have? Wouldn't it be amazing to once again not have to try to be perfect, not have to have it all together, and not give a damn? I mean don't you want to wake up and rock out on life with no requirements?

So, why don't we? What changed?

What the hell happened?

Where's our innocence?

Where's our bounce?

When we were kids, we couldn't care less what anyone thought. It didn't matter. We could look like anything, smell like anything, and do just about anything without reservation or hesitation. But then, it was as if overnight that freedom was snatched away. All of a sudden, everything and everyone mattered, and conformity became law.

Nowadays, we find ourselves considering others in nearly every decision we make. We wonder, what will they think if I do this? What will they say if I say that? This is not to say people and their opinions don't matter, but seriously, who the hell are *they*?

The truth is, there is no *they*, it's *you* and it's *me*. We're the ones judging ourselves long before anyone else gets a chance. The fact that we're even asking these question reveals the real question: am I enough?

"If you live for people's approval you will die from their rejection"
— Lecrae, recording artist/actor/songwriter

CHAPTER 12

CONSUMPTION

Although our kitchen cabinets are full of cups, glasses, and mugs, there are only a few that I actually use. When I use one of my favorite cups, I clean it on the spot, rinse, and re-shelve it. This way, I know each time I go to use it, it's clean and ready for me.

Admittedly, this may be a bit compulsive, and I share this not to inform you of my supreme cup management skills but to highlight a specific moment in the process. I return the cup to the shelf—*empty*.

You'd find it a bit strange if you came over to visit and as you reached to pull a cup from the cabinet, you found it already full of water, wouldn't you? It's supposed to be empty, right? You're supposed to fill it up with liquid after pulling it off the shelf.

This expectation is great for cups, not so much for you and me.

The system of consumption treats us as if we're a glass being pulled down from our kitchen cabinet that starts out empty and then becomes full. Accumulation and accomplishments become the focus of our fulfillment.

Between Black Friday, that has now somehow begun to include Thursday, Cyber Monday and so on, we've reached the point when companies could literally call every day of the week something different, and we'd find a way to oblige. Society sells dissatisfaction. Consumption is our culture's crack cocaine. On your mark, get set, consume.

The U.S. is reporting a positive increase in consumer spending, and this would be great except that the Federal Reserve reported that the same population who is buying what they want (versus need) has more than $3.9 trillion in consumer debt—26 percent of which is revolving or credit card debt.

Just to put this number in some perspective: if it was distributed evenly among all men, woman, and children nationwide, we'd each account for more than $11,970, and that's not counting debt associated with mortgages.

If you don't believe you're adequate before you begin to consume, you'll only end up becoming abundantly inadequate the more you consume.

Look around you. Has there ever been a time in history when we've had such an abundance of stuff and yet such an absence of satisfaction? Our pockets are full of money, houses full of furnishings, days full of errands, calendars full of appointments, and of course, bellies full of food.

So how come our hearts are still so hungry and our souls still starving? We're materially wealthy but physically, mentally, emotionally, and spiritually weary. This system's blueprint is designed for lots of getting but little gratification.

Are you able to sleep at night better with all this stuff? Are you genuinely happy? Are you leaping from bed in the morning, ready to embrace your new day, and embark on a new adventure? Do you now have a more optimistic outlook on life? Are you able to truly enjoy your present without being consumed by thoughts of what else you need to get or do?

I don't need to convince you of anything. Your life is speaking to you, and it's not holding back.

CHAPTER 13

COMPETITION

What are you competing for?

Where did the idea of competition come from?

Have you ever asked yourself these questions?

Once you begin to see **what** you really are, you will begin to see how worthless competition really is.

Once you know **what** you are, you will know that the space you were created to occupy is far too uniquely shaped for anyone else and competition loses its allure.

Compete or Cultivate?

In many ways, the idea of competition is actually a disguised form of intimidation. It makes you think:

Someone's trying to take your spot on the team.

Someone's after your position at work.

Someone's outworking you.

Those are just a few examples of the crap society sells us that causes a competitive spirit. Are they true? They could be, but so what?

You weren't born to compete; you were born to cultivate— from within.

Why be forced into pursuing more than you actually desire? Why allow society to up your ante in life?

Just because the Joneses have something, it doesn't mean you need to keep up. And what has "keeping up" ever gotten you? No really, what does "keeping up" mean in the first place? Who made up these rules? Who's calling all these shots? And, at the end of it all, where's your happiness, which is what we're after anyway, right?

Are you starting to see what I'm saying? We're playing a game we didn't sign up for.

Our very society is passive aggressive, pretending like it's doing us a favor when all it's really doing is dangling a carrot in front of us that we don't even want. It's only because it appears to be the only food available that we eat.

Go harder. Give it all you got. Our society celebrates this sort of approach as it gives the appearance of true dedication and loyalty to one's dreams, goals, and ambitions. We look good to those around us, but when we're alone, the mirror reflects a reality we can hardly stand to look at.

At the age of 14, I entered high school and started playing for our football team. Around the same time, I started watching football more regularly on TV. The Dallas Cowboys with the big stars and blue uniforms caught my eye—and still do to this day. As a player and fan of more than 27 years, I know a little bit about competition.

There's nothing like it: Two teams trying to impose their will on one other, knowing anything can happen at any moment, and only one will go home with the W. As a viewer, my blood is boiling, and my heart is pounding. I'm invested in every snap, and I'm out of my chair every other minute, screaming at the players as if they can hear me.

Their competitive spirit is amazing. These are guys putting it all on the line, risking their health, their careers, and even their lives to defeat their opponent and come away with the victory. Sunday mornings were made for this. Unfortunately, for some people, Sunday seems to come every day.

Do you ever find yourself trying to outperform, outwork, outhustle, and outgrind the next guy as you put in hours trying to get a leg up on the competition?

Listen, I get the whole Beast Mode stuff man. I'm with you on that, believe me. This isn't about not going hard; it's about learning to not go hard for something that doesn't require your effort. I promise you, for every Superman out there, there are 100 Clark Kents saying, "Dude, I'm tired. This shit is too much, I can't keep up the facades. The weight is too damn heavy, my back is about to snap. When will I get a break???"

The issue isn't with you, it's with your criteria and the scale you're using to measure yourself.

Whatever we concentrate on, we magnify; whatever is magnified, we intensify; and whatever is intensified becomes immensely important. The danger in concentrating so much on chasing "greatness" is that we unknowingly run right past some pretty great things in the present moment. We begin to overlook the beauty of what has already happened—*you*.

Dis - Jockeys

At home, at work, in our relationships, and even in line at Starbucks, it's as if everyone, everywhere is jockeying for position and trying to get ahead of the "competition." The phrase "jockey for position" comes from the world of horse racing and describes how a rider tries to get their horse into a winning position during the race.

Spend enough time outside today and I can guarantee you, you'll run into a jockey. At the grocery store, they're the ones staring at you with a smug look as they aggressively pull into the parking space before you. At an event, they're the ones forcing their way to the front. As soon as security opens the gate, they burst in and grab the best seats.

In the business meeting, they're the ones raising their hands to piggy back on every good idea and asking questions they know the answer to so they are the ones most heard. Everywhere you turn, people are maneuvering or manipulating for a "better" position.

Over time, competition has woven its way into virtually every area of our lives. In the workplace, people are no longer people but "resources" that generate successful outcomes for management. Our insecurities convince us that we must protect our turf and that before we can be open to working with others, we must first ensure we're outworking them.

This way of thinking causes us to be restless and even at times ruthless in our relationships. This wasn't why we were created. We were created for cooperation, not competition. We compete not to show others but ourselves that we're sufficient. We believe that if "we win" in a given situation, we'll be satisfied.

They say, "To the victor goes the spoils," but if we were totally honest, we feel just as empty-handed after a win as we did before we started. This is because we'll never get the right result competing for the wrong reason. Hard work pays off unless your goal can't be achieved.

Competition in sports is great but in the context of our daily lives and activities, it's a lie the mind makes up when we're unable to see how sufficient and equal we all are.

Rather than looking for ways to elevate others, we throw them under the bus for fear that we may somehow appear less important if they receive more recognition. We make it about *us*, and this is where we fumble. The game of life is best played with cooperation, not competition. When the team of humanity wins, we can be genuinely satisfied with our success.

CHAPTER 14

COMPENSATION

Ever find yourself feeling stretched too thin or bending over backwards, time and again?

How did you get there? Did you overvalue someone's opinion and priorities and devalue your own? Were you trying to win someone over and get them to notice you or maybe hear a compliment?

The intention is usually harmless but if you are deflated, the result can be devastating.

Overcompensating

*Over*compensating is over committing to an attempt or result. This can be expressed in many ways. Depending on who you are and the context of your life, it will look different.

Are you ripping and running, sacrificing things you shouldn't sacrifice, and giving up things you can't afford for the sake of significance?

You are **do**ing everything you can for everyone you can and leaving nothing for your*self*. You're worn out but you keep finding a way to put on your happy face. When people ask you how you're doing, you say, "I'm good; I'm OK." No, you're not. You're barely holding it together inside.

All this effort and you're still not feeling enough, huh?

You are giving of yourself, your time, energy, and resources with the hopes of compiling a resume of relevance, but it seems as if there is only more empty space to fill. Soon your determination turns to disappointment. You've always believed hard work pays off. What everyone forgot to mention was that in this line of work, you'd be the one writing the checks.

Do you ever feel if you don't accomplish a certain thing by a certain time you'll be a letdown, disappointing other people or your*self*?

Do you ever commit to doing more than you know in your heart you desire, just to keep the peace?

Do you ever find you're going the extra mile to make people happy, only to look up and find yourself walking alone?

*Over-*Owning

As I write this book, my wife and I are renting a house in Southern California—one of the most expensive places to live in North America. And while there will come a time when we'll buy a house, renting is within our ability now

73

and complements our desired lifestyle. My wife, who's a licensed real estate agent and has extensive knowledge of the financial responsibilities associated with owning a home, has helped us avoid its stressful complexities until we are *monetarily* mature to do so.

This being said, what would you think if I told you I've decided to wake up tomorrow, head over to the neighbor's house, and sign paperwork to assume their mortgage payments?

Would you think I was crazy? Would you wonder what's wrong with me? Well, don't worry, I haven't made that decision, nor do I imagine I will anytime soon.

However, a countless number of people make the equivalent of this decision and follow through on it every day of their lives.

Compensation Is *Over*-Owning

I'm sure you've heard of the term "putting words in someone's mouth." Deflation causes us to put other people's words in our mouths.

Just like my renting a home and deciding to take on our neighbor's mortgage payments, owning other people's thoughts and feelings is too heavy a burden for anyone to manage over the course of their lives. And yet we try.

Deflation causes us to look for every possible way to devalue ourselves, even if it means making things up in our own minds. We're looking for evidence to prove that we need to live up to even more.

That's why we take on other peoples' judgments and expectations, most of which they've never even expressed. We convince ourselves that we couldn't possibly have arrived since there's still much, much more for us to do. After all, look at all the criticism we're getting. But wait...whose criticism is it, really? Theirs or ours?

Think about it. Other people never even gave these criticisms to us, we just took them and made them our own. It's like my wife and I renting our house and then informing our neighbor that we will begin paying their mortgage. We own too much, and we initiated the insanity ourselves.

CHAPTER 15

PULLING THE PLUG

"They heard the sound of the Lord God walking in the garden in the cool of the day, and the man and his wife hid themselves from the presence of the Lord God among the trees of the garden."

Today, instead of going to our Creator, our Source, we depend on ourselves for everything. We no longer look for help with anything, including our estimation of enough. Because of this, we carry a burden we weren't built to bear, and we continue to burst our own bubble and poke holes in our balloon.

In life, when you want to stop something from operating, what do you do? You unplug it!

In life, when we want to get away and not be bothered, what do we call it? Unplugging!

What I'm saying is, no matter how you cut it, if you want to put an end to something, you disconnect it. Doing for ourselves meant disconnecting from our Source.

We swapped our satisfaction in producing a relationship with our Source for a satisfaction that prevents a relationship with our system.

Whether in the Bible, or during David's magic trick, once the swap occurred, the deceiver disappeared! Did you notice from the passage there's no further mention of the serpent at this point in the story? It's as if our disconnecting signaled him to perform his world-famous vanishing act.

We're left holding the cards we're dealt and assuming the work of disseminating the lie, which is convincing others to see what isn't there.

The burden of shame, fear, and judgment also are now added to the mix. These all contribute to the concept of *self*-deficiency that, in our minds, requires *Self*-Dependency to resolve.

At its core, deflation is *self*-shaming. Shame is the emotional baggage that we carry not for what we've done but for **what** we are.

I call it baggage because, like anything we carry around, we only feel its weight as long as we choose to carry it.

Baggage can be unloaded, so can shame.

If you recall, in the garden, we had done something we weren't supposed to, but that wasn't our concern. Our concern was what we believed: we were naked.

"Then the Lord God called to the man, and said to him, 'Where are you?' He said, 'I heard the sound of You in the garden, and I was afraid because I was naked; so, I hid myself.'" -Genesis 3:9-10

The phrase "because I was naked" was the answer. This shows us our minds were on **what** we were as opposed to what we **did**. This is the we essence of shame, finding and focusing on what we believe is wrong with us versus others.

This is why it is hard for many people to find true inner peace or what we describe as happiness because there is a lack of congruency between what, who, and why we are. By continuing to give great attention to *who,* which is our personality, and *why,* which is our purpose, without ever discovering **what,** which is our prominence, our lives seem to keep "falling apart." **What** is the glue that holds it all together.

As you will soon see, God loves you so much that He basically says, "Although the world makes you feel like you have to look a certain way or have certain things before others accept you, I'll take you just as you are."

God says, "I see you as you are, with no lies to hide behind, mask to wear or makeup to cover you up. No need for more of anything except for your own acceptance."

A Three-Prong Problem

During the writing of this book, I spent hours in front of my computer to get the job done. I wrote in various places, including Starbucks and the public library. No matter where I decided to write, I needed a three-prong outlet to plug in my computer so its battery didn't die. All three prongs played a role in providing the needed power for the computer to work as designed.

Like my computer plug, individuals have three prongs, and all three play a critical role in supplying our lives with a *surge* of satisfaction.

When we bought the lie and were tricked into reaching for what we didn't need, we not only disconnected from the Source but also from Self and Society. The disconnection was three-fold.

By losing sight of Source, we lost sight of Self, and by losing sight of Self, we lost sight of Society, which is the global community we create collectively. There was a trickledown effect, and it made total sense—defective Source, defective Self, defective Society.

The disconnect began with the questioning of our Source's character and carried on from there.

When the source to something is disconnected, its supply also is cut off. If I was to disconnect my computer plug from the wall outlet, the power would stop flowing. Immediately, the battery icon would appear, and the charge would begin to decline. We are no different.

Satisfaction's power source was cut off when we unplugged ourselves and said to God, "We'll have a go at life with our remaining charge."

Unfortunately, that charge is running low. It's like grabbing your phone off the dresser as you rush out the door for work, only to discover that the battery is barely charged and you left your power cord at home.

SECTION 3
SURGING

CHAPTER 16

PLUG IN TO BEGIN

"Our need to connect is as fundamental as our need for food and water"

— Dr. Matthew D. Lieberman, UCLA

We live in a "how to" culture. As a society, we're stuck on easy step-by-step systems, user manuals and tutorials. It might seem natural for me to provide one of these to you, saying, "Now just go off and follow these cookie cutter instructions, and you'll be on your way to satisfaction in no time."

But I can't, and I won't.

Why? I can't because I don't have the instructions, and I won't because that's not been my experience. My experience, road to rest, recovery, and remarkable reality has been the result of a *relationship*.

As I've said before, all I can give is what I've got. I can share with you what's worked for me and offer it as something that may work for you. As we've struggled with the same problem, perhaps we'll find the solution in the same place.

Reconnecting with my Creator, my Source, is what did it for me. Within this relationship, I discovered what I was looking for. My significance, sufficiency, and satisfaction has always been there; I just needed someone to show me.

As with any relationship, we must learn and adapt to different dynamics and the ways in which we relate to them. In the next few chapters, I want to give you a preview of what I believe you can expect.

Each of these are what I call *"connecting points."* These points are how I saw my Source supplying me with not only what I wanted but also with what I needed in order to see my*self* in a way that satisfied me.

Connect to Correct

Over the last 12 years as a part of corporate America, I've had the opportunity to work as both a project team member and a leader. For deliverables to be submitted on time, deadlines to be met, and the project to be successfully deployed, we always had to connect and connect *often*.

As soon as a new initiative was given, weekly meetings to touch base were set up to ensure we regularly connected and saw the work through to completion.

A necessity to connect is true of every area of life, including our satisfaction in Self.

Try not connecting with food for 46 days—you die.

Allow the grass in your backyard not to connect with water or sunlight for a few weeks—it dies.

How about making some toast for breakfast tomorrow morning without connecting the toaster to the power outlet? Any luck? Nope.

Nothing works without a connection, and the same goes for our satisfaction.

Have you ever failed to pay your electric bill after that third pink slip? What happened?

I know the feeling, walking around in a house dimly lit by sunlight coming through the windows. Electricity is there, it's just not flowing to your house. Everything seems lifeless, the house is full of products, but none of them are working.

The TV sits in your living room but can't play the Red Box movie you want to watch.

The microwave is on the kitchen counter but can't warm up the food you want to eat.

The source has been cut off from what everything depends on to power their purpose.

Our satisfaction, too, depends on our connection to the Source from which it's empowered. The reason systems are so deflating is the fact that we're continuously connecting to a source that is power-*less* to provide what we require.

I'm sure we didn't understand it then but when we plucked that piece of fruit from the tree, we essentially pulled the plug on our power: our Source.

You've got to plug in to begin.

Our Creator is the Source of our satisfaction (in Self) because He's the Source of our significance and sufficiency. And just like anything, when we lose the supply of a natural resource, we must begin to manufacture it. Satisfaction is no different.

In essence, when we reached for the fruit we said, "God, we pass on Your freely supplied satisfaction (significance and sufficiency). We'll just manufacture it ourselves."

The problem is, we threw away the blueprint. We look like God. He's both our mirror and our blueprint. When we cut Him off, we cut off His image and the image of Self. How then can we ever be satisfied with something we can't recognize?

When trying to solve a case, what's one of the first things detectives do? They find eyewitnesses, people who can confidently identify a suspect. How will we know it when we see it?

Why do you think there are so many systems? In other words, why's everyone doin' they own thang?

Consider the national ad campaigns that say, "Just do you." What they're really saying is **do** everything in your power to satisfy your eye.

How's that working for you?

Remember what the serpent said, "[He] knows that in the day you eat from it your eyes will be opened, and you'll be like God...." The implications were that you lack something. You're close but you're not quite there yet. Just **do** a few more things and you'll finally be like God. The truth was, we already were like God.

> *"Then God said let us make man in Our images, according to Our likeness..." -Genesis 1:26*

"God created man in His own image, in the image of God He created him; male and female He created them." -Genesis 1:27

The lie was an idea that we weren't enough in our present state. For me, the biggest eye opener was realizing that the attack wasn't against what we had but **what** we were.

CHAPTER 17

RELATIONSHIP

Before I begin to discuss reestablishing a relationship with your Creator, I want to address the elephant in the room.

For many of us, the pressure cooker we call "culture" has aided in corrupting the very concept of a relationship. Some of you are thinking to yourself, "My whole life, all I've even seen is breakups, divorce, and back stabbing so what the f--k is a relationship, seriously?"

I see where you're coming from. I get it, believe me. Born to two teenage parents, I watched my mother become addicted to alcohol and crack cocaine, and struggled to become a man without my father in my life. I was sexually abused by family friends, emotionally abused by family members, ridiculed by classmates, and intimidated by unstable teachers. I had my heart broken several times by girlfriends with whom I felt I had serious connections and could trust, so I know a little something about the reality of rough relationships.

Today, I've found true love, acceptance, and most important, happiness in God. I now understand none of these people intentionally hurt me; they just couldn't see my value because they couldn't see their own.

I've grown to forgive each of them and pray for them because I've been shown the brokenness of humanity. There are no lower, middle, or high classes. We're all in the same class(room) of chaos and confusion. We're all struggling to understand and learn true love.

In our society, love is treated like a casual four-letter word. The very idea of truly trusting someone has become an outdated exercise. Marriages come with prenuptial agreements, business contracts come with fine print, and goods and services are sold with specific terms. Shall I go on? Where's the trust?

This may be challenging for many of you—it was for me. But that doesn't change this lesson's importance. Just because we ruined the reputation of relationships, it doesn't mean they are no longer relevant.

Just because we've misused one another doesn't mean we're not useful. And just because we've had horrible experiences in the past with relationships doesn't mean we can't decide to create better ones in the future.

Once you begin to reconnect and reestablish your relationship with your Creator, He begins to reveal your relevance. He'll be reestablished as the Source of your significance, sufficiency, and satisfaction in Self.

You'll be empowered to "fail" yet feel like a success. I know it sounds crazy, right? I know your experiences up to this point have been the complete opposite—when you failed, you felt like a failure. I get it, I've gone through it. But when this relevancy really becomes your reality, it becomes a new way of thinking and seeing everything.

Re-Learning 2 Love

The greatest achievement imaginable is to achieve nothing and yet appreciate ourselves as if we've achieved it all.

Has anyone ever given you something you didn't earn or even deserve? Can you remember the surprise, joy, happiness, and satisfaction you experienced in that moment?

OK, now take all those emotions and all that gratitude and multiply it by million. That's the love of God, His acceptance and appreciation, or at least the best way I can describe it.

This is what you get to experience every single day within a relationship with our God, our Creator. That's been my reality for several years and why I'm so excited to offer the insights of this book to anyone willing to consider something radically different. This relationship is the place where you'll find the rest you require and the satisfaction you've been searching for your whole life. Your happiness is in His hands!

Love Can Only Exist in a Relationship

Love is a word used to express our feelings, emotions, and beliefs within a relationship. Whether you feel you truly know what love means or have identified a "placeholder" in your heart until the next best idea of it comes along, I want to offer what love has become for me since reconnecting to our Source.

I want to share this with you because the purpose of this book is ultimately to help you see the significance of **what** you already are.

In my experience, the only thing that allowed me to see this was a loving relationship. Sometimes, it takes looking through someone else's eyes to finally see what you've been missing.

My current definition of love is "enduring actions expressed through an enduring appreciation." This definition is based on both a verb and a noun, a behavior and belief, for several specific reasons. I believe our Creator opened my eyes to see these things so I could begin to see what I'd been looking for.

In the world of finance, appreciation (which is defined as recognizing the full worth or implications of something) refers to the increasing value of an investment. The way I see it, God has invested you and me into the world so if I say I love you and appreciate you, your value should always be increasing in my eyes.

When I say, "I love you," I'm beginning to filter that statement through my paradigm of love. I admit, I'm learning to love. To love myself and love others. I'm humbled by the idea that I don't fully recognize my worth nor do I fully understand yours.

But this is not a bad thing. In fact, it's *great*. This means the rest of my life can be a process of learning more about me, more about you, and more about humanity as a whole.

"For God so loved the world, that He gave His only begotten Son (Jesus) that whoever believes in Him shall not perish, but have eternal life."
-John 3:16

"Greater love has no one than this, that one lay down his life." -John 15:13

Once I saw a love like this, I saw a sacrifice (action) spurred on by significance (appreciation). Notice that in both ways, there's a sacrifice from one for the significance of other. I'm sure God is not sending His Son to die for a world in which He sees no value or significance.

"In this is love, not that we loved God, but that He loved us and sent His Son (Jesus) to be the propitiation for our sins." -1 John 4:10

This is our Creator saying, I know you all turned your back on me but I'll never turn mine on you. Jesus was the ransom for your recovery. Jesus died for you before you knew him, not once you did.

Do you see what's happening? Seriously, let's think about this. Someone's willing to send their own flesh and blood to die for you and you've done nothing for them, and on top of this, the person sent to die for you willingly agrees to it. This shows me I'm *enough*.

If your Creator sees that you are enough before you've done anything to deserve it, who are you to require anything of yourself before you feel enough? You didn't have to earn God's love and appreciation. Why should you have to earn anyone else's love and appreciation, including your own?

Who are you to think you don't measure up when your Creator has made it clear that you're His, and everything that's His measures up? Stop looking at what you didn't do, He says, and look at what I've already done.

Our Creator didn't wait until He met you to decide this. Unlike relationships in life where you're pressured to live up to someone's expectations, with our Creator you are enough because you exist.

Even though I turned my back on Him in the garden, like a newborn baby cutting their own umbilical cord and telling their parents, "I got it from here," He wants me, welcomes me, and acts to restore our relationship. Like a man who's been served divorce papers, He continues to send his ex invitations to the chapel where He stands ready to renew their vows.

I know there's all kinds of love out there but this is the kind of love I want to be involved in. This is a type of love I want to release and to receive, to give and to get, don't you?

At this point, let me give you a word of warning. You may want to earmark this page by folding down the top corner or, if it's an eBook, you can use yellow highlights. Either way, you may need to revisit what I'm about to say many times over as you journey into a restful relationship with God.

Because our perspectives are like habits and hard to break, it's very possible that you'll try and relate to God like you relate to others and to yourself. I did.

You're so used to exhausting and earning yourself you may try this with God, and He's not interested. He knows your resume, and your history has no impact on how He sees you today. We're the only ones keeping score and counting our wrongs against us, not Him. I know society expects Superman, but God knows you're Clark Kent and He wants to be the Super of your Man.

A coworker of mine, Tony Attallah, once shared a great point with me about our culture.

"We tell each other we should learn from our mistakes, yet we chain people to their past," he said. "Our last interaction with them leaves a lasting impression that creates a belief and barrier that's nearly impossible for them to overcome, even if they've improved."

The crazy thing is, we treat ourselves the same way. We condemn ourselves and see our present through the eyes of the past. We aren't allowed to simply fail; no, we must become failures. See the difference?

This isn't the case with God. Of course, it will take some getting used to, as with any new or revived relationship. Even if you've believed in God your whole life, relating to Him like this may feel new so this is important to keep in mind.

CHAPTER 18

(*SON*)DAY MORNING

My relationship with God began on a Sunday morning siting in the Toledo County Jail. Booked on theft charges, I found myself in an all-too-familiar place. It was the weekend so I wouldn't see the judge till Monday. Time was dragging, and so was my life.

After breakfast was served, the deputy came by our cell block and announced that church service was available for anyone who wanted to attend. I knew about church, but I was not religious. I had a vague idea of God, but it was nothing serious and certainly nothing you would consider a relationship. Still, I wanted out. Even if the church service was only for an hour, I thought that would be an hour not spent staring at the walls of my 6 x 9 foot cell.

I agreed to go, along with about 10 other guys from the cell block. We all walked down the hall to a little room not too far from the cells that held no more than maybe 15 people. There were four tables with three chairs each and an area in front with a chalkboard. I remember there were two or three women from a local church all wearing white dresses and hats. I don't recall everything they said but I do recall them talking about a man named Jesus who died for our sins and their inviting us back into a relationship with Him.

At some point near the end of their message, they asked all of us to put our heads on the table and close our eyes because they wanted to pray for us and didn't want anyone to be distracted.

As they began to pray, they asked, "Are you tired of where you are?"

"Do you want to change and life to be better?" they asked. "If so, make a decision and raise your hand."

As if it moved on its own, my hand was in the air before I could even process what was happening. I was broken. I had no fight left, and I knew in that moment if I didn't do something different my life would continue to go downhill. I was desperate to see things change. I didn't realize it then but the thing that was about to change was me.

I didn't know anything about deflation or self-sabotage. I didn't understand that my destructive behaviors signaled a return to my deflated beliefs about who I was. Back then, I had no faith or insight into any of the things I'm sharing with you in this book. No, back then I was just a lost, hurt, and emotionally wrecked young man looking for something better, looking for refuge from all the pain I was experiencing. That day I found it...or I should say, Him.

94

The lady asked everyone with their hands up to take one more step of faith and come up to the front. Again, without hesitation, I stood up. Without remembering how I got there, I found myself at the front of the room, bent over slightly with my hands in the air, and a woman's hands on my shoulders praying for me.

She said, "Say this, 'Lord Jesus forgive me (for **do**ing things my way). I want you back in my life. Live in me and through me.'"

While I'm sure there was more, this is the little I can recall, but this little meant so much.

Are you at this place in our life? Are you thinking, I'm tired of being overlooked, I'm tired of being overworked, I'm tired of being overwhelmed, or just tired? I can't keep living this way. I'm at the end of my rope. I've tried everything I know to *do* and it's not working. I'm not satisfied with my life or with myself.

If you are, I want you to know that you and I are no different. I've felt the same way. I was under the same pressure, suffered the same pain, and cried the same tears.

I want you to know that the One who created me is the One who created you. He loves us the same and will do the same for you as He's done for me. The relationship, relief, and *rest* I've received, you can, too.

You, too, can "come up front" and lift up your hands right where you are, right now, and simply say, "Lord Jesus forgive me (for **do**ing things my way). I accept you back into my life."

If you just said this prayer, I want you to understand something: You have been reconnected to your Source of significance. Your relationship has begun, you are *connected.* Your relationship with God your Creator has been reestablished, and you will soon begin to see things you've overlooked for years.

It's really that simple. Accepting Jesus is a *heart* condition, not a hand condition. Using our hands is what got us in trouble in the first place.

Two words—"I believe"—with heartfelt conviction is worth more than two hours of heart-*less* chatter. Even prayer is often used as another system. What was meant to cultivate a relationship can easily be used as a way to create results. If we're not careful, we will turn the relationship with our Creator into another chore.

Jesus represents God's help. Jesus represents God's way of helping us reconnect with Him and recover our *in*sight, the sight we lost when we set our sights on the tree.

Essentially, when you accept Jesus, you accept God's help. You make a conscious decision to no longer go on your own at this thing called life, happiness, and satisfaction.

Although Jesus means a lot more than this and, in this pivotal moment in my life, certainly did a lot more, right now I simply want you to think of it as, "When I accept Jesus, I accept God's help, and I am making a decision with the conscious recognition that I want to see things, most importantly myself, the way God does."

God has always and will always see you as enough and wants nothing more than to help you see that. He helped me. He'll help you, too.

Now, just as a heads-up, rarely will something "magical" or dramatic happen in this moment. I know we're a spectator society, always looking to be wowed, but just know it takes time to develop a deep appreciation for God and for yourself. Unfortunately, time appears to be something we never seem to have anymore. Don't let that be the case for you. Just as hard as you've worked to become enough, work to see that you already are enough.

After being released, the first thing I did was run into the open and accepting arms of my local church, the First Church of God in Toledo, Ohio, where Associate Pastors Kerwin and Madelyn Manning became my spiritual parents. They connected me with groups of people who loved me as I was, including Brother Vincent Wiggins, who welcomed me into his home and would pray with me. He cared for my soul and mentored me.

Pastor Kerwin also began to take me to breakfast on Saturday mornings, where he opened the Bible and answered any questions I had. God surrounded me with many great people who helped me grow and mature in life to the place I am now.

I suggest you do the same. If you're not part of a Bible-believing church, start to look for one. Tell them your story and get plugged in. Don't go at this alone; get connected to a community of people that can support you through this process. You weren't created to figure everything out on your own. There are many great men and women God has grown and matured, and they are waiting to embrace you as they did me.

You might have tried this before and gone to church only to find it wasn't what you expected. Maybe you were offended or even treated poorly by its members. Try not to let a few people's mistakes cause you to miss your miracle.

Remember that we are all imperfect and all suffering from deflation to varying degrees or at particular times. Please don't throw out the baby with the bathwater. Good, trustworthy people do exist.

Just as you're discovering in this book, our value is unknown to us and many times when people treat us badly, it's because they don't understand our value, let alone their own. No, that doesn't make the offense any less painful. I'm not giving them an excuse, but I am offering you an explanation, one you can choose to accept and use to move forward.

Don't let rejection by others prevent you from renewing your relationship with God.

A Relationship You Can Feel

Relationships are critical because you are more likely to believe information shared by someone with whom you're in a relationship versus someone you're not.

Think about it. Through relationships, we build our trust and confidence in the words and actions of others.

Did you ever need something but didn't feel comfortable asking certain people? Or, have you ever been walking down the street and felt uneasy when passing a stranger? These are our natural tendencies when we lack trust, trust that only comes as a result of a growing relationship with someone.

If God says you're an amazing individual but you're not in a relationship with Him, how likely is it that you will believe Him? Until we come into a relationship with the One who says you're enough, you'll continue to trust in the words of the one with whom you are in a relationship—usually yourself.

This is why deflation is considered *Self*-Dependency. You're depending on *Self* for your information about *Self*. But because *Self* didn't create *Self*, it has no clue how to properly assess nor answer your questions and provide information.

Before I move on, I want to be extra clear about something: This isn't about getting you to come to church on Sunday, to read your Bible every day, and be a good little Christian. This is about returning to a *relationship* that you walked away from, and renewing your connection to and confidence in the only One who knows **what** you're made of.

I'm not the Sunday "Secret Service." There'll be no tickets issued or jail sentences here. Your relationship is *your* relationship. You know whether you're in one or not; it's not mine to monitor. And while I'm at it, let's be clear that I'm not about playing games and making our relationship with God a strict ritual or some sort of Christian checklist.

The organized Church (Sunday morning service, Sunday school, weekly meetings, etc.) was an entry point for me and remains a vital part of my life. But it was and is the personal relationships that I developed that made the difference.

For fear of overlooking someone, I won't mention any specific names other than my spiritual father, Pastor Kerwin, who took me under his wing both literally and figuratively. He met with me one-on-one at a Denny's restaurant in Toledo for more than a year.

There's a saying that "in some cases, you'll be the only Jesus some will ever see," and Pastor Kerwin was being my Jesus until I was mature enough to know Him for myself. Our weekly meeting *was* church, it was ministry, and it was a relationship based on an acceptance and appreciation for **what** he saw in me, not what I could **do** for him.

Since then, several strong men in the Church have mentored me in one season of life or another, and to them I am eternally grateful. They know who they are.

I share how my relationship with God came to be because it is my sincere hope and prayer that you, too, encounter such personal expressions of appreciation from God and others.

The You God Created

This relationship is unlike any other as you will not only be getting to know your Creator but His creation—you.

Think of it as getting well acquainted with yourself. He already knows everything about you. He created you so there's no need to try and prove yourself to Him or earn His love. He decided you were acceptable before He even formed you. The very thought of you was enough. That's why you're here.

This also goes for anyone saying to themselves, "I've always believed in God. I pray every morning and have been going to church every Sunday since I was three years old." That still doesn't mean you've ever entered a real and restful relationship with Him.

Going to church on Sunday doesn't mean you're in a relationship with God any more than going to a bar means you're on a date.

"Be still (stop striving) and know that I am God."
-Psalm 46:10

CHAPTER 19

READY TO RECEIVE?

Just as the tree holding ripe fruit releases it to you, requiring no great effort on your part, so will you receive revelations of **what** you are.

> *"(Come to me, all you who are weary and burdened, and I will give you rest). Take my yoke upon you and learn from me, for I am gentle and humble in heart, and (you will find rest for your souls). For my yoke is easy and my burden is light."*
> *-Matthew 11:27-30*

This is about understanding what you're really looking for and realizing it's (you've) always been there.

God is inviting you; yes, *you*. To you, the one reading this book right this moment, come and feast on the fruit of your fulfillment. Come sit, be satisfied, receive the *rest* you've been longing for.

No system, no sweat, no stress. No assembly required.

From my personal experience, the best way I can describe these moments of revelation is that they are moments of clarity and conviction. These moments are so convincing and so compelling that they cement a truth within you that can't be broken. Once He opens your eyes, you'll never want to close them again.

Of course, that's not to say every day is rainbows and ice cream cones, but it is to say that what you know about you, you'll *know*. *N*o matter what the day brings to you, you'll bring **what** you are to it and you will **be** enough every time.

Calling all deflated souls, all those who've been overlooked, overworked, and overwhelmed: You can come right now and learn to let go of everything that's ever caused you to see yourself as anything other than enough. Come discover the secret to your satisfaction.

Just because something has yet to be revealed doesn't mean it doesn't exist. Is it possible that there are things about you (including your significance) that can exist yet be unknown, even to you?

Revelation: a <u>secret</u> or <u>surprising</u> fact that is made known.

Revelation is a look inside—insight-<u>full</u> information.

Revelation is a breath of fresh air. The breath you've been wanting to take for soooooo long.

The Bible says, "Then the Lord God formed the man of dust from the ground and breathed into his nostrils the breath of life; and the man became a living being." (Genesis 2:7)

We get the concept of inspiration from this image of God's blowing into and inflating man. This is how I see revelation. The man was simply a shell of himself before being inflated.

Do you feel like a shell of yourself, like you exist but have no excitement about your existence? When God reveals, He releases a breath that revitalizes. And when He shows you something only He can show you, you're inspired all over again. Your soul is refreshed and rejuvenated.

You literally feel alive again.

Seeing Is Believing

If you believe something, it usually means you've seen it. However, not all seeing is done with our physical eyes. Some seeing (and often the more important life-changing type of seeing) is done with internal (*in*)sight or perception.

If you don't believe you are enough, it simply means you don't see enough of you. You're all there. In fact, you are more than you could ever desire or dream of, but of course that means nothing if you can't see it.

Seeing in this sense is seeing not with your eyes but with your heart. Oh, you didn't know your heart had eyes? What do you think sees your dreams? Your vision? Your Creator? Human eyes weren't created with the capacity to see beyond the physical and tangible things right in front of them.

This is where God's revelation comes in.

For example, a couple is expecting a child and elects not to find out the sex of the baby before birth. The day has arrived. The baby passes through the birth canal and only the doctor knows it's a boy. Does the couple's lack of knowledge change the gender of their child? No.

Oh, but wait, there's more. Once the doctor says, "It's a boy," the parents now know the gender. But guess who's still in the dark? The child himself. For the first several years, this baby will live, breathe, eat, sleep, and do all things healthy little boys do. Yet he doesn't actually know he's a boy until a later time.

You're that baby, **do**ing what you know to **do**, but not knowing **what** you are.

Picking Up the Pieces

Think of your*self* as a jigsaw puzzle with all the pieces ready to assemble in the box. You're complete in that aspect. You just need a little help putting it all together so the picture can be seen. God through His revelation wants to help you piece your portrait back together. The one we tore apart with our own hands in the garden.

Motivational speaker and author Jim Rohn says, "Happiness does not come from what you get but from what you become." Well, in my opinion, the only becoming we need to **do** is becoming aware of **what** we already are.

The same is true of you. Before and at the point of conception you were **what** you are and **what** you are is enough. It just wasn't revealed to you.

To give you an example of God's revelations and share a bit of what you can expect in your relationship with Him,

I'll show you one of the things He revealed to me during the course of writing this book. He showed me how the place of rest is not only *your* goal but also *His*.

A rested soul is a rested person, a person with whom God can do great things and to whom He can entrust great things, including revelation. A rested person is not easily manipulated by society because a rested person has found satisfaction in and of themselves; they're not looking to someone else for approval nor are they depending on anyone for it. A person at rest isn't needy or wanting or easily deceived by conniving people.

Rest is a powerful and power-*full* position because your confidence is cemented not by what you can do or get but by what God has already done and has already given. This results in an unshakeable satisfaction.

As God our Creator, He is blessed tremendously to see His creation at rest. It says to God, "I trust you with my life and my situation." Rest is the greatest compliment you can give Him.

Rest also is showing the world that your soul is saying, "I believe that what God has made me to be is enough."

Our rest is a result of our revelation.

Revelation is about seeing more, not trying to be more. This may sound strange but you are now all you'll ever be and there's nothing wrong with that because all you'll ever be is enough.

The truth, in my experience, is that we don't become more of anything, we simple see more of what's already there.

Revelation is all about revealing what you and I have spent so much of our lives overlooking. It's about allowing God to do what He desires, which is to reveal to you what amazing things exist today so you're free from having to expect so much of tomorrow.

This is why our systems don't suffice. Significance is not something you get, it's something you're given. When God begins to reveal you to you, you may be tempted to turn your attention to what you've done or what's to be done to you. You may think, how in the world can I possibly be that great?

Remember that your behavior and the behavior of others in your life is based on beliefs. This misuse does not provide reliable indicators of your value. I've driven down the street and seen expensive Mercedes-Benz cars that look like they haven't been washed in months. Their state of cleanliness, however, says nothing about their inherent value.

Who's better qualified to show you your significance than the One who gave it to you?

Without our Creator revealing **what** we are to us, we're left making things up as we go. Sure, we can come up with a few things we'd like to consider ourselves, but let's be honest, how's that working so far?

By reverting to make-believe, we create more work for ourselves while God wants nothing more for you than what you want for yourself. He wants you to know you're enough, to be satisfied with your*self,* and to rest in the revealed knowledge of **what** you are.

Work was intended to be an enjoyable expression of our significance in the world, not the evidence of it.

The reasons systems fail to satisfy is that they fail to appreciate. Appreciation is something that must be given by another, and true appreciation can't be manufactured or made up.

One million make-believe affirmations can't compare to a single act of authentic appreciation. There's just something about being appreciated by someone else without having to act on their behalf, and that's what we get with God.

The Bible says that before we even knew Him, God sent His Son Jesus to redeem us, the very people that turned our back on Him. That's saying a lot about you, and I think it reveals you're enough.

Because he knows you, our Creator will reveal things to you in a way you can understand, grasp, and receive. You are so unique, special, and significant that God refuses to cookie-cut His love for you. He'll relate to you creatively and personally. When the student is ready, the teacher appears.

Are you ready for a lesson in *rest*-ology?

In our systematic society, it's important that I keep it real about revelations and inform you upfront that there are no rules about how God reveals things to you.

Some people are shown things through their dreams.

Some people will read something like this book, and the light bulb will come on.

Some people are told things at critical moments in their lives and it just *connects*. This is what happened with me 17 years ago when Pastor Eric said, "You are a teacher."

That simple statement changed everything. It revealed not only **what** I was but also the specific way I could contribute to society and impact others for the better. I can't really explain it. You just know and when you know, you *know*.

These are all forms of revelation, and I'm sure there are a million more He can use to reveal things about you to you.

Please don't put limits on how you can receive His revelations. Resist the temptation to overthink or overcomplicate or (if you've been in this relationship for a while) over-spiritualize it.

The bottom line is that a revelation is simply something revealed. Something shown to you that you hadn't previously seen.

SECTION 4
SELF (HELP)

CHAPTER 20

WHAT A *WONDERFULL* LIFE

Many mornings, I have to wipe my eyes and clean myself up before heading into work because I've been crying the whole ride. My face and shirt are soaked with tears, not brought on by fears and frustrations, but by unspeakable joy, gratitude, and happiness.

It's an amazing feeling to know that, before I do a single thing or say a single word, every day of my life I am loved and accepted and appreciated. I don't have to perform for anyone or meet anyone's expectations. Rest has become my reality and it can become yours as well. I mean, who wouldn't want this life?

It's amazing to continually experience an indescribable excitement just because you exist—not because you "executed perfectly" or "came through in the clutch," etc. but because your very existence is remarkable.

This reality is what I stand for. This is what I'm "selling." This is my "product." I can't promise you one million dollars. I won't tell you that every day will be full of sunshine. But I can tell you, and I will tell you, that with God's revealed loved and appreciation of you at the forefront of your mind each morning, nothing and no one will ever again rob you of your rest. There will be no more struggling or striving to prove to others what you're made of. You'll know **what** it is, and it is enough.

The overload is OVER!

I'd like to continue by sharing with you the same inspiring and insightful ideas that were shared with me. These are ideas that have helped me see **what** I am and understand that **what** I am is, has always been, and will always be, enough. Seeing **what** I am has helped me to both reach and reside in a state of satisfaction with my*self.*

It is my belief that these ideas, when considered with an open mind and a bit of creativity, will help cultivate a confidence within you like none you've ever imagined so that you, too, will find personal satisfaction, relief, and rest. Your happiness is at the helm!

What's the Big Deal?

I'm glad you asked. Otherwise, you may have never known this isn't a question as much as it is a statement—a big statement.

What *is* the big deal? Knowing **what** you are makes all the difference. Depending on **what** we *believe* we are, we will think, speak, and act a certain way. Last time I checked, these three things are the sum total of our life experience. What people call their lifestyle is really their belief-style.

When I know **what** I am, I know what I should and should not be **do**ing. Knowing **what** I am frees me of the burden, pressure, and weight of unrealistic expectations set by self-imposed idealisms. I don't have to tell you, you already know how draining it is to run around doing everything asked of, offered to, and suggested for you.

Let's say I'm a car that thinks and speaks. Yes, a car. (I told you, you'll need a little imagination and creativity to roll with my ideas.) But in case you need a little help, just think of Lightning McQueen from the children's movie, *Cars*.

As I was saying, I'm a thinking, speaking car designed to comfortably drive four passengers. If 10 people want to ride in me, I don't have a problem saying no. I don't feel bad for them and I won't allow them to make me feel bad about myself. I wasn't constructed to carry that load; it's not work I need to be concerned with doing.

Does that make sense?

For many years as a person, however, I worked hard, completing things but never feeling complete my*self*.

I believe the reason for this is simple: If you don't know **what** you are, you don't know what you need. If you don't know what you need, you'll spend your life accumulating or accomplishing a lot of things but none of it will be satisfying.

The greatest thing you will ever become is accepting of **what** you *already* are.

What Are You?

Answer that question and ask yourself honestly, did you like the answer? Was it extraordinary, exhilarating, and energizing?

I find that when I ask most people that question, the answers I get are pretty typical. Most will answer with one of three things, including their gender, job title, or social role (e.g. mother, father, wife, husband). It's not that their answers aren't true but that they refer to an obvious identity and don't reveal a true *Self.*

It reminds me of a popular song that came out a while back by the artist, Rag'n'Bone Man (Rory Charles Graham) called, "I'm Only Human." The chorus lyrics are, "I'm only human after all/Don't put the blame on me," and the song has been used in several nationally televised TV commercials, movies, and advertisements.

I don't know about you but I don't want to be *only* anything. I want to know that my life represents much more than one thing—and not more things I believe I have to **do** but things I believe I *already* am.

Don't you?

"Imagination is more important than knowledge. For knowledge is limited to all we now know and understand, while imagination embraces the entire world, and all there ever will be to know and understand."

— Albert Einstein

I find that our imagination when it comes to *Self* is much too bland; deflation has dulled our description, like when television could be viewed only in black and white. Although the world had always been bursting with vibrant colors, we watched a reduced version of reality. The issue then was not with the world but with our ability to see the images as they really were.

Why shouldn't your very existence excite you?

Who says you can't be your own inspiration?

This is what will happen when God begins to reveal you to you. When you start to see your*self* in full color, you'll never settle for black and white again.

Maybe what you've been waiting for is what you've always had. Maybe what you've been wanting to become is **what** you've always been—enough.

The more I became aware of how deflation works, the more I realized how it infects our imagination. At first, you may not think the imagination is a major part of all this but soon you will see just how major it is.

The imagination is continually used and will project one of two images, either how great we are or how great we're not. It's like going to the movies, where we're all staring at a jumbo-sized screen while behind us a little machine projects images of a motion picture.

See where this is going?

In the same way, your little projector called imagination will take the idea of not being enough and forecast jumbo-sized images of all the reasons you need to **do** more and more and more. Being conscious of this helps us understand that these images are not absolute and were created months, even years, before we saw them.

Looking back to when I was a child growing up with a poor self-image, I can confidently say I was pressured into projecting pictures of myself as something less than acceptable before I ever had a chance to understand and accept **what** I was.

Everywhere you look, you're inundated with images of "perfection" and popularity trying to distract you from your true *self*-interest and discouraging your true *self*-investigation.

I used to think that society stole our imagination. But our imagination hasn't been taken, it's been tainted. Poor ideas about *Self* project poor images of *Self*.

Guess-timations

My wife and I recently celebrated our 18th wedding anniversary after 20 years together. After getting married at the ripe ages of 23 and 18, respectively, we've both had many different jobs and tried our hand at several career paths. When I first met my wife, she told me she was inspired by Jody Foster's character in "The Silence of the Lambs" and wanted to become a forensics detective.

While I never understood why anyone would want to be around dead bodies and crime scenes all day, I never discouraged her from following her dreams. But in time, her ambitions changed, and I'm glad they did. Even though she would've been the one performing the investigations, just knowing she was literally "staring death in the face" on a regular basis would have been difficult for me.

I share this memory because I believe when it comes to identifying **what** we are in terms of our value and significance in the world, we often make what I call "*guess*-timates" that only superficially explore *Self*.

Human life is fragile and complex, and **what** we are is not always obvious. It is, in most cases, hidden under the layers of lies from our past and often painful experiences. We've committed a crime against *Self* that requires a thorough investigation. This is no time for *guess*-timates.

As future freaks, we've been so possessed by the importance of making progress that we often make quick decisions about things. The problem is that we apply this approach to ourselves and make uninformed decisions about **what** we are. It's the difference between looking at a situation and looking into a situation.

When I *guess*-timate, my conclusion is based on what appears real to me. When I investigate, my conviction is based on what the evidence reveals to me.

It's like when someone presents you with important information and you don't have time to dedicate to it right then. You'll say something like, "Thanks, I'll look into that." What you're saying is, I really value the information being presented, and want to invest adequate time and energy to ensure I make a fair and quality assessment.

Are you living a *guess*-timated or an investigated life?

I asked, "What Are You?" But what I was really asking was, "What do you believe to be your origin, identity, worth, value, use, importance, purpose, and significance?"

This is why seeing and believing **what** you are at this very moment is so critical to the satisfaction or *happy* you seek. To be satisfied is a present tense expression. It means to (already) have enough, to (already) be enough—not soon, not someday, but *right now*.

Seeing through revelation **what** you are allows you to begin living *from* your value versus living *for* your value. Learning **what** you are means learning what you can begin to express, experience, and enjoy the present.

God wants you to know that **what** you are is resolved and affirmed. You're His resolution and His result. While the world is caught up on trying to evolve, God wants you to know that the best version of yourself is not the Self you can achieve tomorrow but the *Self* you can accept today.

Learning **what** you are and not what you may be someday allows you to finally take a load off. By knowing **what** you are, you'll discover you're enough and knowing this sets you free from the burden of believing you have to do anything to earn it.

Uncharted Territory

Seeing **what** you are is about seeing your*self* in ways you've never explored.

You're like a Russian matryoshka doll; as soon as you open one doll, you discover another, and the search has just begun. When you stop at the outer shell, you are robbing yourself of the enjoyment of experiencing the entire exploration process to find out **what** you are.

This is why these revelations (or *in*sights) are so satisfying; with each new discovery, you experience a new expression of God's love toward you. It is this love, this revelation, this knowing that someone cares for you unconditionally—no prejudice, no prerequisites—that affords you relief and allows for the rest you've been looking for.

When you begin to see **what** you are, you see that each day is not only a gift to you but that you are a gift God has given to each day. When people ask, "Who do you think you are, God's gift to the world?" You'll start to say, "Yes! Yes, I am!"

You'll no longer simply start your day but you'll embark upon it, embracing it as an adventure rather than a tiring endeavor. You'll stride through the front door with conviction, wondering how God will use what you are today to influence, impact, and improve the lives of those around you. You'll enter each day believing that you're enough for all people, at all times and in all situations. You'll no longer work *for* your worth but work *from* it.

Appreciate What You Are

Seeing **what** you are is seeing what you mean to society as a whole. In other words, humanity needs you.

This isn't arrogance, which is a form of fear and insecurity but humility at the highest level. Humility is being secure in your God and in your*self*. Humility is believing what God believes about you.

For generations, we've been taught to focus on figuring out who we are or why we are without ever learning to appreciate and confidently articulate **what** we are.

What is the missing link. **What** supports who I am and shows why I am. **What** solidifies the value of *Self*.

CHAPTER 21

CREATION

"Then God said, 'Let us make mankind in our image, in our likeness'...So God created mankind in his own image, in the image of God He created them; male and female He created them."

I know many theories exist about the origin of mankind, how we got here and whether or not there's a higher being (God). I respect that yet I have to say that in my 41 years, I've tried believing in just about everything, and didn't receive my personal satisfaction and rest until I believed in God the Father, Son and Holy Spirit—our Creator.

The emphasis is on Creator because Creators think, plan, and execute with purpose.

"...all things are created twice. There's a mental or first creation, and a physical or second creation to all things"

— Stephen R. Covey, The 7 Habits of Highly Effective People

Our Creator dreamed of us and engaged His great imagination in creating us. There are no duplicates—not one. Even paternal twins are different in some form or fashion, and that's amazing. That's also part of what makes you so amazing.

We are made in His likeness by His imagination, and that is something we should not overlook. Seriously, we should all be in awe of one another. We are the product of God 's imagination. Let that soak in for a minute. We're His vision.

Created with Purpose

Understanding that you are a **creation** means knowing you have a very distinct and intentional reason for existing. There's no Big Bang or Evolution crap here. Your very existence is both spectacular and specific. There are no mistakes or osmosis; there's nothing but pure and particular purpose for you.

Created things serve a specific purpose.

Created things fill voids.

Created things solve problems.

Created things bring great joy and pleasure to their creator. (In this case, our Creator.)

Solving a Problem

The value of anything that is created is generally not recognized until it is experienced and helps ease a problem that it was designed to solve. It made it possible to accomplish something. This is why I say people are a solution to a problem, too.

You're both God's invention and society's innovation. You're an upgrade, an improvement, and a breakthrough. This is why knowing **what** you are is so satisfying. You know that you belong.

Breakthrough has become a popular term among those in the church as well as self-help and psychology industries, but the truth is, your birth was a breakthrough.

Many of us are sitting around waiting for a breakthrough, not knowing our very lives are a breakthrough. If we were able to see that, we'd have much less waiting around to do.

Purpose and Pleasure

One of my simple pleasures in life is a late-night bowl of cereal—Golden Grahams, to be exact. I know I shouldn't but hey, I'm purposed, not perfect!

I'll grab the milk, cereal and bowl, then…wait, what's missing? If you answered a spoon, you're correct. Why not a knife or a fork? Because the spoon is specifically designed to meet the demand.

I don't know the history of spoons, but I do know the history of creation and that things start as inspiring ideas. At some point, the idea occurred to someone for a tool that could scoop and hold, not cut or poke. Through careful thought, planning, and production, the spoon went from idea to invention.

The result: problem solved, and many people satisfied, including me.

If something exists in the world today in physical form, it means that at some point it began as an idea. Ideas are the most profound and priceless commodities known to mankind. Everything began as an idea, including you.

The Lightbulb

My family and I go to the movies a lot, and one of my favorite animated features is the "Despicable Me" series. I love it because of the character, Gru. Besides all the hilarious havoc he wreaks in the world, Gru inevitably gets a devilish grin on his face and declares with great confidence, "Lightbulb."

Gru says this when an idea has come to him, a vision of how he's going to pillage and plunder.

This is how I envision God when he thought of us, minus the devilish grin. But the confidence and passion Gru expresses when the thought pops into his head is what I believe God experienced when He thought of us. God said, "Aha! I've got it. I have an amazing idea."

God said, "Let us make mankind in our image, in our likeness," before he said, "Let us make man." He had to first think that there was a need for Me to make man.

Did you know that before you ever became an individual in our society, you were first an idea in the mind of our Creator? This means, you serve a significant purpose in the world.

Ideas change the world, and so have you. The world is already better because you're here.

Ideas represent solutions to problems and so do you.

Ideas provide answers to questions and so do you.

You are an inspired idea.

Try something for me: Look around you right now, no matter where you are, and pick something, anything. OK, got it? Now, if you were to google that item followed by the word "inventor," it's likely that a lot of information would pop up that would start to point you in the direction of the item's origin.

To test my theory, I did a quick search myself. As I looked up from my computer, the first thing I saw was our dining room fan. My google search revealed that an American electrical engineer, Schuyler Skaats Wheeler, invented the first electric fan in 1882. He had been envisioning for some time what we would eventually see.

The need for fans appeared before they were invented, and their significance became clear because they were in high demand.

We are no different.

What I'm suggesting is that being an idea is perhaps the greatest thing you and I could ever believe we are. This statement may sound a bit odd at first but the more you consider how ideas are formed and how they function, it starts to make sense to see your*self* this way and to acknowledge just how significant you really are.

In order for an idea to emerge, there must first be a need. In other words, ideas "hear" the cry of pending questions and unresolved problems, and come running to save the day.

You-nique

Again, I'll ask you to pause for a moment, no matter where you are, and to focus on any object you see. I promise you, it's an answer to a question or a solution to a problem. I'm serious, go ahead, try it.

Point to anything, and ask yourself the questions: Why does this exist? What is this being used for? What does this allow us as a society to do or enjoy what we previously couldn't?

The answers to those questions help you understand the inventor's intent and why they got the idea to create that object in the first place.

Now, consider its design, shape, color, and mechanics, etc. I mean, really examine it and think about all the elaborate details that went into its formation. Think of the hours of thought, research, and development it must have taken to finally bring this object into existence—from mind to material.

At some point, a person asked the question. They likely started with some of these opening words: I wonder. What if. There should be a way to. I wonder how.

And an idea came to be.

A part of your significance is what you have (gifts, talents), but it's not so much what He placed in your hands as what he placed in your heart that is the center of your contribution to the world.

The way you are is the why you are, and you are needed and wanted just as you are, as envisioned by God when He created you. Therefore, as our Source's idea and our society's answer/solution, you can confidently see that you have significance and always will.

What we are is the significance for which we were sent.

What we are is the prominence that preceded our arrival.

What we are is the unchanged, unaffected, unaltered use.

It's amazing to know that no matter what others may say, think or do, your identity in this world is the very idea our Creator had in response to a question at the heart of humanity or a problem suffered by our society. Yes, that's what you are.

CHAPTER 22

CONTRIBUTION

Someone asks, "What's your problem?" and we think we've usually done something to offend or upset them. They want to know what's going on. But here, I'm asking what problem in the world has become *your* problem?

In other words, we all know the world is full of problems. The morning news provides a fresh list to choose from each day, but what specific problem, when you see it, does something to you on a personal level?

You're able to see some things in a way that makes them impossible to ignore, they captivate you and "call" your name from out of the crowd. This is what countless heroes in history experienced when they saw injustices and were compelled to act to contribute to the cause and correction of a problem.

What is it for you? What gets under your skin and makes your heart beat a little faster when you see it? That thing that just came to mind may be a clue to the contribution you were created to **be**.

You may be thinking to yourself, how can I be a contribution? I understand being a contributor, meaning I give something to a cause or charity, but my being a contribution *myself* is hard to grasp.

OK, think of it this way: Have you ever seen those TV shows where they interview a rich kid who has everything in the world materially yet found a way to spiral out of control? Maybe they've started using drugs and eventually become depressed. Usually, they talk about how their mom and dad provided all these things but all they ever wanted was their love, their attention, their presence—them.

Relationships keep popping up because they are central to human existence. There is no true satisfaction without relationships, we're created for them. We are created to express (release) and experience (receive) appreciation for what we are within a relationship with God, ourselves, and each other.

This is why knowing **what** we are allows us to rest and receive the happiness and satisfaction we're searching for. When I know **what** I am, I know God appreciates me, I appreciate myself, and I appreciate others, knowing they, too, are God's contributions to society.

When others witness this sort of appreciation happening in your life, they will be inspired to join in and appreciate you as well.

No matter what specific ways God chooses to reveal you to you, in my experience, it will be in the form of a contribution.

You may think you're already contributing, ripping, and running all day, doing everything for everybody. You're right but that's the problem. Being a contribution doesn't mean being an errand runner or a "yes" man or woman. It means allowing your existence, not your efforts, to be of assistance to others.

Look at it this way: Doing all that is tiring. What you may be calling "contribution" actually is just a bunch of work. Work can be done by just about anyone but a contribution takes the right one to do it.

To one person, all that running around is fulfilling but for another person, it's draining. Just because you're doing *a lot* doesn't mean you're doing what's *right*. Remember, deflation is focused on earning enough. It's concerned with quantity—i.e., the more I **do**, the sooner I get to *be* enough.

Doing everything is a sign you have yet to be shown what you are to *Self* and to others. Without the insight of revelation, you'll continue to overload your*self,* and remain overworked and overwhelmed. Does this make sense?

Once you know **what** you are, you know what you are supposed to be doing or not doing and, in that revelation, you will find rest and be satisfied with *Self.*

In our society, we're used to things like, "I'd like to contribute to…," which paints a picture of some sort of gift we give to someone. I'd like to invite you to expand your view of contributions and consider that you, in and of yourself, are a contribution. You are a sort of gift.

You are a solution to a problem, an answer to a question. What if your satisfaction isn't achieved in changing what you are but in allowing **what** you are to change everything around you?

There is nothing better or more satisfying than to contribute (give) as you were intended. Just as a baseball bat wants to hit home runs and help a baseball team win the Worlds Series, we instinctively want to contribute and help someone "win" in an area of their lives.

Doesn't it feel great when you're able to help someone out and they express their appreciation? That is when you know for sure that you, just the way you were created, are enough.

What's Your Sign?

When I ask about your sign, I'm not talking about a horoscope. I'm talking about what you stand for and what you show the world when we look at you.

You are a sign. No matter who you are or where you are, what you have or don't have—you *sign*ify something spectacular.

Let me ask you something: When was the last time you were in your car? Picture yourself driving down the street. Did you reach your destination? And at some point during the drive, did you encounter a traffic light? Yes? And what happened? Did the yellow light make you slow down? Did the red light cause you to stop? Did the green cause you to start up again? Yes? Why is that?

Because they are *signs*.

Each color indicated something, didn't it? Your adherence to these signs showed your appreciation for what it signified, and the benefits it afforded you, and the passengers of your vehicle.

These signs prevent accidents, provide direction, and maintain order in what could be an otherwise chaotic traffic situation.

The colors are universal indicators so well engrained in our culture and psyche that we now use the combination of red, yellow, and green in many other ways. When we see these colors, they trigger very specific thoughts, feelings, and actions.

Like a traffic light, your life provides our society with vital information. It is a sign that will prevent problems, provide direction, and establish order in the lives of those who pay attention. You show us where to get something we would never have been able to find without you.

"For since the creation of the world His invisible attributes, His eternal power and divine nature, have been clearly seen, being understood through what has been made, so that they are without excuse."
-Romans 1:20

Do you have any special talents, gifts, abilities, or know-how that seems to come naturally to you? Are there particular things you do well or feel deeply about? Are there things no one has ever really taught you but sort of come easily for you? Are there certain problems in the world that bother you but others that you seem able to tolerate?

Consider this: the problem we're most clearly able to see is often the clearest indication of the solution we were created to **be**.

A Double Shot of Significance

I have spent many, many hours at Starbucks. The coffeehouse chain has become a writer's best friend with free Wi-Fi and tables with built-in power outlets, caffeinated coffee, and a nice assortment of goodies to fuel a work session. It also has free ice-cold water, which is great because hydration is key to optimal brain function and focus for a mental marathon like writing a book.

Starbucks has become so dominant in North America that it's difficult to drive more than two or three blocks without seeing their green-and-white sign. Even as a frequent customer, I have no idea what the logo of the little woman with stars around her head means. What I do know, though, is that it signals my writer's paradise. Of course, there are other options but they don't have nearly as many locations.

Let's use our imagination (again) and pretend like the Starbucks' sign could speak. You ask it the following question: "When people see you, all they think about is coffee and computers. Is that really enough for you?"

How do you imagine the Starbucks sign would respond?

I think it would say, "I feel amazing. Coffee and computers are exactly **what** I was created for. My Creator dreamed that one day I'd stand tall and proud, signaling to people of every race, color, and creed where they could have a great cup of coffee and get some work done. I don't need to show people where they can find burgers, or pizza, or gasoline. All I need to do is stand here and shine brightly so when people see me, they know it's coffee time."

Do you see where I'm going with this?

The Starbucks sign is completely content, satisfied with itself as a sign for coffee and computers. Isn't that what we're all really trying to do? To be like this sign, and to find a way to be OK with what our sign says.

This is what God wants: For you to be completely satisfied signifying your true purpose. Once He revealed this to me, I've never been quite the same. I know that I'm absolutely amazing because I was created to show people something only I have the ability to show them. Competition doesn't exist in my world; no one can "out signify" me. I'm the only sign like me. Period.

It's so hard to put into words just how awesome it feels to be shown your sign, even for a writer. It's so liberating. I am free from the systems of people pleasing, fitting in, or living up to anything for anyone. Society has lost its ability to make me feel bad for not meeting its standards. I only have one standard now and that's the one my Creator assigned me—to be **what** I am.

This is not arrogance. It's appreciation.

Remember, appreciation, not accumulation, is the appropriate approach to satisfaction and overall happiness.

Look, I get it. In a world where very few have the ability to appreciate themselves, it sounds a lot like arrogance. What do you mean you're important? Someone in your position? What do you mean you're amazing? Someone who's never had this or that? What do you mean you're significant? Someone who's never gone to this place or that place?

If you were to ask me, "How it is that I can think of myself as being so great?"

In reply, I would ask you, "How is it that you figure that I am not? What are you looking at to draw your conclusion?"

Obviously, not me. You couldn't possibly see me and think that I'm anything less than significant or anything less than spectacular. And the same holds true for you. There's no way I can truly see you—the you whom God created—and think of you as anything less than amazing.

This is the outlook of a person to whom God revealed their sign. I've seen my contribution, and it is to help you see yours.

So, take your foot off the pedal of your prominence. You're at the intersection of life—the red light just turned green. Go. Stop waiting for tomorrow, you are the only sign you need to proceed.

Your Creator doesn't wait until you've accomplished something before appreciating you. Why should you?

To see **what** you are is to see the "green light" of life. With each new day, you get to wake up to a new possibility rather than a prison, a freedom rather than a fear, and a hope rather than a hindrance.

You start to fly with no wings, climb with no hands, and run with no legs. Things you once thought you needed you need no more, and things that controlled you no longer have a hold on you.

You are no longer deflated by a system that makes your significance subject to change, whether it's your situation or the people around you. With all that change happening, how would you ever be able to appreciate what's real? Ahh, that's the point, you wouldn't.

Listen, I don't know about you but I don't want to live the rest of my life with inconsistency, going through life never settled and never stable.

Knowing that you are a sign with a contribution to make is knowing no one has any influence on that: Not the world, not your family, not your coworkers. No one has any say. Never again will your value be in question. Nothing can manipulate, minimize, or marginalize your significance in this world. Nothing will have the power to steal your satisfaction or hinder your happiness.

Contribution remains no matter what, even if your situation or circumstances change. Whether you are rich, poor, popular, or an outcast, it doesn't matter because it's not dependent on anything or anyone's opinion. Your happiness persists.

Birthed Because

> *"Before I formed you in the womb, I knew you, and before you were born, I consecrated you; I have appointed you a prophet to the nations." -Jeremiah 1:5*

Never doubt your importance. The fact you exist is the evidence that you are something our society needs. Our Creator said, "Society has a problem, so I'll send the solution called 'you' to be the solution."

Once you see your sign and yourself as a contribution, you'll no longer look to construct a life for your*self* but instead contribute a life *from* yourself. In other words, your effort is no longer used to "get a life" but to give one.

We're born into a world that trains us to see ourselves as something that starts off empty and needs to be filled when the truth is—we're full needing to be emptied.

In its most important sense, contribution signifies —and that means *enough*. In the traditional sense, people are able to make contributions to things like charities because they have enough to cover their bases and provide for others. The idea is, there's enough to go around.

Seeing yourself as a contribution is seeing yourself as sufficient, as enough, and to be enough is to be satisfied. Satisfaction is a product of allocation, not accumulation.

CHAPTER 23

RESTED

"You can lead a horse to water, but you can't make them drink."

— John Heywood's "Proverb Collection of 1546"

I certainly don't consider you a horse (or any animal, for that matter), but the above proverb certainly applies to all of us.

I can show you how to lighten your load, and where rest and happiness is found because it's something I've experienced and a road that I've traveled. I can walk you right up to the door but you must open it. Ultimately, you will need to decide what to believe.

Rest is ultimately a resolution.

"Therefore, let us be diligent to enter that rest..."
-Hebrews 4:11

The fact of the matter is, God our Creator is the Source of our value, worth, and significance—our *enough*-ness. He wants nothing more than to build a loving relationship with you where He can reveal more and more of the wonderful **what** He's created you to be. The door of rest has swung wide open but you must decide to walk in and take a seat.

Let me be the first to say that it's not the easiest thing in the world to take this step but neither is continuing to live a deflated life. Now that you've been exposed to both sides of life's coin, you no longer have to flip it and hope it lands on the side you want. Now you can make an informed and inspired decision.

Let me be completely honest with you: The only reason rest is difficult to enter is because it means leaving your control at the door. Have you ever boarded an airplane and seen the sign that says certain items can't be brought on beyond a certain point? If so, you know that it means you have to let go of something you may be carrying (control) to get to your destination. You feelin' me, right?

Control Is a Crime

The greatest crime we ever committed was the one against ourselves. While we were busy robbing the tree of what didn't belong to us, we overlooked the fact that we were being robbed of what did belong to us—namely, our relationship and our rest.

We think we want control but we really don't. Control is too heavy for us to carry. Our backs weren't built to bare this burden. We give it all sorts of names and label it various things: Pressure, stress, fear, anxiety. They're all symptoms of our struggle with deflation. We're witnessing the weariness of life without rest.

We're overwhelmed and our souls are drained. Such extreme exhaustion was never God's intent for His creation. Did the concept of work come from God? Absolutely, but the way we do it did not. Working for our worth and our *enough-ness* is a complete perversion of God's plan for our lives.

Your soul is starving for stillness. Yet your inability to relinquish control robs you of your own rest. Rest requires resolve. You have to decide to leave behind the old (controlling Self) and embrace the new (relinquishing Self).

Our ability to rest depends on our ability to relinquish control of results and allow God to release to us what we need when we need it, based on **what** we are and why we are. This will be different, and this will be challenging, but it will also be absolutely liberating.

"Cease striving and know that I am God." -Psalm 46:10

If you strive for something over any significant period of time without seeing the results you're looking for, you will eventually grow weary and begin to experience physical, mental, and emotional exhaustion.

The key word here is exertion. This is striving; it's not just working but working yourself up. This isn't to say there's anything wrong with hard work but there is when a) you don't believe it's OK to take a break every once in a while, and b) all that effort is for earning something that isn't earned but learned.

In this context, rest is an internal mental, spiritual, and psychological position from which we operate our lives. Your body may be at work but your soul isn't stressing and straining to see what's already there.

Rest is the state of enough, and enough is the state of rest. You're returning to a place you may have never seen but has always been your home.

Rest is your residence—the summer home that's been bought and paid for with all your work but you haven't had time to visit in a while.

Rest is the difference between working *for* significance and working *from* it.

Rest is a sign that symbolizes the work has already been done. For you to see your significance, you must see that you've met the requirements. But rest is knowing you're prequalified, like a successful mortgage application or credit card application with your name preprinted on the label.

Enough already has your name on it. The work was finished a long time ago. No more results are required.

Wrestling with Results

Results are the reason you can't rest. They are out there somewhere ahead of you, and you always feel you need to catch up to them, right?

Josh Guerrero, my life coach and an amazing humanitarian and leader, taught me that anxiety is attached to anticipation or the expectations of things to come.

If you live by or for results, it's no wonder you find it difficult to slow down, take a break, and enter His rest. Results are meant to be a part of your life, not life itself. Does that make sense?

It makes sense to me because it wasn't too long ago I was there, and if I lose focus of this truth, I slip back into it. We all will from time to time. This is why knowing you're not a failure is so important. When you slip back, you'll remember not to mistake yourself for the issue.

"Remember that failure is an event, not a person."

— Zig Ziglar

We live in a world deflated by its inability to appreciate the internal values of the human existence. It's a world where our value systems operate on what a person (including you and I) can **do** rather than **what** a person can be.

When we rely on our results as a way to prove to ourselves that we're enough, as I was doing, we essentially become enslaved to our own expectations. Sounds crazy, huh? But we do it all the time.

The Unexpected

By definition, an expectation is hinged on what someone or something will do—always future tense and pending. Our value, worth, significance, and satisfaction are always being postponed as if our remote control of reality is on pause.

Expectations are not bad things. They just shouldn't be used for something that's already occurred.

Rest is the difference between people who work for the results and those who wake up knowing they are the result.

What's ironic about the whole rat race is that you can be so obsessed with getting results that you overlook the one result that matters most—YOU.

Did you know that you are a result? Yup, you are. You're God's result.

> "Then God said, 'Let Us make man in Our image, according to Our likeness; and let them rule over the fish of the sea and over the birds of the sky and over the cattle and over all the earth, and over every creeping thing that creeps on the earth.'" -Genesis 1:26

Just think about that for a moment; let that sink in. God wanted you, and you're here. Now, say it to yourself, "I am God's result. I am what God wanted." How does that feel?

When you begin to see yourself this way, everything changes. Knowing you are a result is knowing you'll never need to work for it. That's a total game-changer.

We're chasing results but what we need and unknowingly want is a single relationship.

Your Life Re-Imagined

Imagine for a moment what kind of life you would live if you believed that you were just as significant, important, and valuable before you did a single thing as you were after you did everything.

Imagine the person you'd be if nothing could ever again prevent you from completely accepting yourself and believing that you were enough for anyone and any situation?

Imagine life with no pressure to perform for others or to be the best at anything.

Imagine being relieved of the unrealistic expectations you've put on yourself for years.

Imagine you are free from your past, once and for all.

Imagine being able to fall flat on your face (I mean, completely miss the mark, foul it up, and get it all wrong). But no matter how badly you "failed," you didn't consider yourself a failure.

How would that feel?

How would you live differently?

The truth is, that's the life God has always had in mind for you. He wants your rest as much if not more than you do, but you need to take your hands off the wheel and allow Him to navigate the needs of your life.

Rest and Rewards

Our rest is the greatest compliment we can give God because it says, I trust Him. Whenever we cease to fight and willfully rest in the control or care of another, it communicates to them the highest level of confidence we can afford.

Let's see what this looks like.

Take a moment right now and close your eyes. I want you to imagine you're on a boat and all of a sudden, a horrible storm blows in, and you're thrown overboard by the crazy winds. The waves look like walls, and they come crashing down on top of you, one after another. Try to feel the impact. The water is overwhelming, and you've lost any sense of control over the situation. You're starting to drown.

You're taking in huge gulps of water and feel yourself choking, unable to breathe. You attempt to find the boat and wonder if you can grab it, but the water is coming too fast, and you're no longer able to see anything.

You begin to work desperately to stay afloat, and just as you are about to give up, you hear a faint voice saying, "Stay calm, stop panicking." It's the Coast Guard, and they are telling you to stop struggling and relax. They are not asking for your help; they don't need your strength or your effort. For them to do their job successfully, all they need you to do is stop.

Like breaking any bad habit, learning to do less will be challenging at first. You've been doing so much for so long it's become both your lifestyle and way of life. It's all you've ever been taught, all you've ever heard, all you've ever seen, and it's the only way you've known—until now.

I know I said I don't have any "how to's" for you but if there is one, it's learning How to Take A Load Off.

What if I said, the hardest thing in the world to do is rest?

Would you think I was crazy?

That I was out of my mind?

Would you think, "Shoot, that's not hard at all. I can do that with my eyes closed—literally."

Well, not so fast. When most people hear the word rest, they get images of being in their beds at night or lounging around on the living room couch with their legs kicked up on the coffee table. And while that's one picture of rest, the picture I want to paint is the one of your soul, not your body, at rest.

Deflation is an *over*working and *over*loading of one's soul, interfering with the mind and internal peace. It's not being able to rest in the idea of being enough at all times, no matter the situation or circumstance, and it does not allow us to be satisfied with ourselves.

Deflation is the drained mind, saying "I gotta **do, do, do** or I'll never **be, be, be, be**."

The truth is, you've been thinking the same way for years so changing it may take years. In fact, it's going to take the rest of your life. Opposing ideas will never cease to present themselves to you.

Every day you wake up, you'll be presented with new opportunities to rest or resort back to the old way of seeing things. The idea of resting in the reality of our relevance versus "reaching" for it is completely countercultural.

"When you change the way you look at things, the things you look at change."

— Tony Robbins

When we rest, we get to experience a life we never would know had we worked for everything. Setting goals and achieving them is good, there's nothing wrong with that, but when it comes to being enough, there's nothing like the crown of contentment that can be received only from our Creator.

"Not that I speak from want, for I have learned to be content in whatever circumstances I am."
-Philippians 4:11

In other words, if I have a lot or if I have little and do a lot or do a little, I'm good. Regardless of my situation, regardless of my circumstances, regardless of my result, I've learned the secret to always being enough.

Content is another way of saying, "I'm happy."

Often when you say, "I'm not happy" or feel dissatisfied, it means you feel as though something is missing, lacking, or outstanding.

Being content means being satisfied, and being satisfied means you come to the place of rest. This is why revelation is the key. God wants to teach and wants you to learn contentment in Him and in you.

Rest is learned, not earned.

CHAPTER 24

A HELPING HAND

"[All] those things that we think we are, feel limited. I'm not enough, not worthy, I'm scared; ... the only thing we have as evidence of that is our past. I'm not enough because that one time..."

— Kyle Cease, author and actor

Your thoughts can't define you but they can deter you. They can dominate your day and send you on a whirlwind of destructive dialogue that ends in self-disgust.

This has happened to me more times than I can count. This also is why writing this book was not an option. I know I'm not alone.

This is where God met me and wants to meet you, and it's at this point that we not only need a better sense of Self but a sustaining and satisfying one.

Time to Pick a Self

Some things you just have to try for yourself.

As much as I have described this life to you, you'll ultimately need to try Him for your*self*. All I can tell you is that there was once a time in my life when I literally fell asleep and didn't want to wake up the next day. Now, I can hardly sleep through a full night because I'm so excited to start the next day.

> *"Taste and see that the Lord is good; blessed is the one who takes refuge in Him." -Psalm 34:8*

Satisfaction or happiness is a choice. All of us must consider these new ideas about Self and make a choice to be content. Satisfaction isn't something that comes to us after we've done enough to earn it.

Being satisfied is something we must choose to be, at any time and in any situation. Armed with this great information, you will ultimately be the deciding factor in whether it's rhetoric or reality.

Being satisfied with Self is living in a state of satisfaction. Unlike geographic states like California or Ohio, this state is internal. It's a state of mind or a mindset. It's an internal residence where we must resolve to reside and from which we must refuse to be evicted.

That said, I know some of you will want to point the finger and make it about someone else. I did for years.

Everyone else's reactions were the needles on my *enough-ness* meter.

We'll look for ways to make someone else's attitude or behavior the cause of our pain and, by doing so, we divert blame and avoid owning this decision. I get it (been there, done that), and the truth is that you can choose to stay there.

As I've said from the beginning, this book is an offering you certainly can refuse to accept. I only ask that you pause for a moment and ask yourself the question, "What kind of life could I live if I allowed no one else to determine how I felt about myself ever again?"

The truth is, people hurt other people and deflated people deflate other people. I know there are some pretty serious crimes committed against us as a society, many of which I've suffered myself, so I'm not in any way belittling your experiences. I feel your pain. I just want to express that people only have the power we give them—nothing more.

This book is about doing less, letting go, releasing control, and unloading unnecessary weight from our lives. Why not include those you're blaming and holding accountable for your suffering? Holding onto the past and making others responsible is still holding, and last time I checked, holding is a lot of work—work that'll never be worth the effort.

Because our struggle starts with us, so must our satisfaction. We cannot wait for society to appreciate us. It's time to stop depending on the approval of others, even those closest to us. It begins with you. Trust me, once you begin to see your value and live in a way that shows it, others will see and follow.

It always comes down to us to decide what we'll believe, embrace, embody, express, and experience. Depending on what we choose, we'll either reside in a state of satisfaction or remain stuck in the struggle.

My intentions are simply to inform you of inspiring ideas that can help teach you about your*self* and to invite you to consider them as your own.

In my 41 years, one thing I've learned is that I can't force my perspectives on anyone else, and I wouldn't want to. These ideas have to fit and flow naturally, and I can only offer them to you.

"Self-worth comes from one thing—thinking that you are worthy."

— Wayne Dyer

I am not reaching out my hands to pull you closer to me, for I am in the same boat as you. No, my hands are instruments I've resolved to relinquish to the service of placing your hands in His. He's the One and only One that can give you rest and show you enough of your*self* to be satisfied and find the happiness you desire.

We've journeyed together over many pages, and it doesn't end here. This is simply a fork in the road, and I look forward to seeing you on the next leg of life.

Until then, may you be rested in your soul and satisfied in your Self.

ABOUT THE AUTHOR
TREVEAL C.W. LYNCH

Treveal C.W. Lynch is a certified personal trainer, ordained minister, mentor, inspirational speaker and author of The Corridor to Confidence, released in 2008.

With extreme passion and transparency, Treveal has been captivating audiences for over 18 years. Through his thought-provoking yet highly applicable messages, Treveal has become known as "the voice they listen to." As a trusted communicator in both the business and faith-based community, Treveal continues to present innovative ideas that spark the imagination, inspires the soul and calls for lasting life change!

Follow Treveal at www.iamthepossible.com or on social media @iamthepossible.

CPSIA information can be obtained
at www.ICGtesting.com
Printed in the USA
FSHW021116040120
65623FS